By Robert Lowell

Land of Unlikeness (1944)
Lord Weary's Castle (1946)
The Mills of the Kavanaughs (1951)
Life Studies (1959)
Phaedra (translation) (1961)
Imitations (1961)
For the Union Dead (1964)
The Old Glory (plays) (1965)
Near the Ocean (1967)
The Voyage & Other Versions of Poems by Baudelaire (1969)
Prometheus Bound (translation) (1969)
Notebook 1967–68 (revised and expanded edition, *Notebook*, 1970)
History (1973)
For Lizzie and Harriet (1973)
The Dolphin (1973)
Selected Poems (1976) (revised edition, 1977)
Day by Day (1977)
The Oresteia of Aeschylus (translation) (1978)
Collected Prose (1987)
Collected Poems (2003)
The Letters of Robert Lowell (2007)
Selected Poems (2007)

NOTEBOOK 1967-68

Robert Lowell
NOTEBOOK 1967-68

FARRAR, STRAUS AND GIROUX
NEW YORK

Farrar, Straus and Giroux
18 West 18th Street, New York 10011

Copyright © 1967, 1968, 1969 by Robert Lowell
Introduction copyright © 2009 by Jonathan Galassi
All rights reserved
Distributed in Canada by Douglas & McIntyre Ltd.
Printed in the United States of America
First published in the United States in 1969 by Farrar, Straus and Giroux
This paperback edition, 2009

Library of Congress Control Number: 2009927451
ISBN: 978-0-374-53210-9

Designed by Betty Crumley

www.fsgbooks.com

1 2 3 4 5 6 7 8 9 10

for HARRIET

Even before you could speak,
without knowing, I loved you;

and for LIZZIE

Contents

Introduction

Notebook 1967–1968 appeared in the spring of 1969, at the height of America's tormented struggle over the Vietnam War. Harvard University, where Robert Lowell was teaching, experienced violent demonstrations, the occupation of university buildings, student strikes. It was a time of ferment in politics and social mores, and *Notebook* partakes of that sense of daring and possibility. With its aura of frank, even anguished, experimentation, of self-questioning and yearning, the poem epitomizes its moment as much as Norman Mailer's *The Armies of the Night*, in which Lowell himself plays a central role, albeit in a very different key.

In the late sixties, Lowell was the undisputed dominant figure in American poetry. When his previous book, *Near the Ocean*, came out in 1967, he had appeared on the cover of *Time* magazine—which put him at the apogee of fame for a writer—and his involvement in antiwar politics, his patrician air and comfortable inhabiting of the role of the poet as public man, contributed to his mystique. *Notebook 1967–68*, though, shows us another Lowell: private, casual, provisional, risk-taking in his attempts to catch feeling and thought on the fly. Contemporary events play a relatively minor role here; as the poet wrote in his "Afterthought" to the much revised and expanded edition published in 1970 as simply *Notebook*, it "is less an almanac than the story of my life."

He had been finding new ways of telling this story all his career. In *Life Studies*, published in 1959, he had developed a fresh, understated, prose-influenced style that had changed American poetry. Now, a decade later, he was once again breaking away from an established rhetoric, reaching for something more immediate and impressionistic—what he referred to first as "surrealism," and then, more accurately, as "unrealism," a way of writing "loosely in touch with reason" that "eats from the abundance of reality." The result was a long, digressive, piecemeal work composed of unrhymed fourteen-line "sections" of blank verse, some few with the finish of major lyrics, many others occasional and unpremeditated and, at times, obscure. As its title indicates, *Notebook 1967–68* has the jotted-down, "opportunist," "inspired by impulse" quality of a private document. Once again, Lowell—challenged perhaps by what he regarded as the excessive freedom of Ginsberg and the Beats, and by other anti-formalist gestures in the poetry of the moment—was finding his own way of testing the boundaries of organized expression. As he had written to Elizabeth Bishop back in 1959, "My trouble seems . . . to be to bring together in me the Puritanical iron hand of constraint and the gushes of pure wildness." Here, constraint was loosened as perhaps never before.

Lowell had hit on an endlessly expandable form, and it proved irresistible. He revised about a hundred of the original "sonnets" in the 1970 *Notebook* and added more than ninety new ones, "scattered where they caught," he explained. "I couldn't stop writing, and have handled my published book as if it were manuscript." The process continued for years. Eventually, with the help of Frank Bidart, the *Notebook* experiment resolved into two books: *History*, a greatly expanded version of the public sections of the original, and *For Lizzie and Harriet*. These were published in 1973, along with *The Dolphin*, a sequence of sonnets about the poet's relationship with Caroline Blackwood, who would become his third wife. These works are included in Bidart's edition of Lowell's *Collected Poems*, but there was not room for the earlier *Notebook* versions as well.

Bidart writes in his introduction to the *Collected Poems* that as Lowell worked on making *History*, he "seemed incapable of resting with anything as provisional in feeling and texture as *Notebook*." He shunted the personal material of the original off into a book of its own, and, "alone, in [his] Plutarchan bubble," concentrated on creating a public work that would "cohere," a capacious, grandiose, quasi-Victorian structure that attempts to encompass the entire world (an ambition that Bidart suggests had underlain Lowell's work all along). Bidart also tells us that "Lowell in the end didn't think of either book as replacing the other, and hoped both would remain in print."

Because of its searching excitement, *Notebook 1967–68* demands to be read on its own, and it is for this reason that we are reissuing the poem (in the July 1969 second printing, which added two sonnets to the first edition). In its unconstrained, provisional, off-the-cuff looseness, its quicksilver, sometimes uncomfortable reaching for fleeting perceptions, it marks a significant moment—perhaps the most revealing of all—in Lowell's ever-evolving approach to his art.

—Jonathan Galassi

NOTEBOOK 1967-68

Harriet

1

Half a year, then a year and a half, then
ten and a half—the pathos of a child's fractions, turn-
ing up each summer. God a seaslug, God a queen
with forty servants, God . . . she gave up—things whirl
in the chainsaw bite of whatever squares
the universe by name and number. For
the hundredth time, I slice through fog, and round
the village with my headlights on the ground,
as if I were the first philosopher,
as if I were trying to pick up a car
key . . . It can't be here, and so it must be there
behind the next crook in the road or growth
of fog—there blinded by our feeble beams,
a face, clock-white, still friendly to the earth.

2

A repeating fly, blueblack, thumbthick—so gross,
it seems apocalyptic in our house—
whams back and forth across the nursery bed
manned by a madhouse of stuffed animals,
not one a fighter. It is like a plane
gunning potato bugs or Arabs on the screen—
one of the mighty . . . one of the helpless. It
bumbles and bumps its brow on this and that,
making a short, unhealthy life the shorter.
I kill it, and another instant's added
to the horrifying mortmain of
ephemera: keys, drift, sea-urchin shells,
packratted off with joy, the dead fly swept
under the carpet, wrinkling to fulfillment.

(3)

3

An unaccustomed ripeness in the wood;
move but an inch and moldy splinters fall
in sawdust from the aluminum-paint wall,
once loud and fresh, now aged to weathered wood.
Squalls of the seagulls' exaggerated outcry,
dimmed out by fog . . . Peace, peace. All day the words
hid rusty fish-hooks. Now, heart's-ease and wormwood,
we rest from all discussion, drinking, smoking,
pills for high blood, three pairs of glasses—soaking
in the sweat of our hard-earned supremacy,
offering a child our leathery love. We're fifty,
and free! Young, tottering on the dizzying brink
of discretion once, we wanted nothing,
but to be old, do nothing, type and think.

4

To summer on skidding summer, the rude spring rain
hurries the ambitious, flowers and youth;
the crackling flash-tone's held an hour, then we
too follow nature, imperceptibly
change from mouse-brown to the white lion's mane,
to thin white, to the freckled, knuckled skull,
bronzed by decay, by many, many suns . . .
The child of ten, three quarters animal,
three years from Juliet, half Juliet,
already ripens for the night on stage—
beautiful petals, what shall I hope for,
knowing one choice not two is all you're given,
health beyond the measure, dangerous
to yourself, more dangerous to others?

(4)

Long Summer

1

At dawn, the crisp goodbye of friends; at night,
enemies reunited, who tread, unmoving,
like circus poodles dancing on a ball—
something inhuman always rising on us,
punching you with embraces, holding out
a hesitant hand, unbending as a broom;
heaping the bright logs brighter, till we sweat
and shine as if anointed with hot oil:
straight alcohol, bright drops, dime-size and silver. . . .
Each day more poignantly resolved to stay,
each day more brutal, oracular and rooted,
dehydrated, and smiling in the fire,
unbandaging his tender, blood-baked foot,
hurt when he kicked aside the last dead bottle.

2

Humble in victory, chivalrous in defeat,
almost, almost. . . . I bow and watch the ashes
blush, crash, reflect: an age less privileged,
though burdened with its nobles, serfs and Faith.
The possessors. The fires men build live after them,
this night, this night, I elfin, I stonefoot,
walking the wildfire wildrose of those lawns,
filling this cottage window with the same
alluring emptiness, hearing the simmer
of the moon's mildew on the same pile of shells,
fruits of the banquet . . . boiled a brittle lobster-
shell-red, the hollow foreclaw, cracked, sucked dry,
flung on the ash-heap of a soggy carton—
two burnt-out, pinhead, black and popping eyes.

(5)

3

Months of it, and the inarticulate mist so thick
we turned invisible to one another
across the room; the floor, aslant, shot hulling
through thunderheads, gun-cotton dipped in pitch,
salmon, when lighted, as the early moon,
snuffed by the malodorous and frosted murk—
not now! Earth's solid and the sky is light,
yet even on the steadiest day, dead noon,
the sun stockstill like Joshua's in midfield,
I have to brace my hand against a wall
to keep myself from swaying—swaying wall,
straitjacket, hypodermic, helmeted
doctors, one crowd, white-smocked, in panic, hit,
stop, bury the runner on the cleated field.

4

The vaporish closeness of this two-month fog;
thirty-five summers back, the brightest summer:
the Dealer's Choice, the housebound girls, the fog;
fog lifting. Then, as now, the after curfew
boom of an unknown nightbird, local hemlock
gone black as Roman cypress, the barn-garage
below the tilted Dipper lighthouse-white,
a single misanthropic frog complaining
from the water hazard on the shortest hole;
till morning! Short dreams, short shrift—one second, bright
as burning shavings, scattered bait and ptomaine
caught by the gulls with groans like straining rope;
windjammer pilgrims cowled in rubber hoods,
making for harbor in their yellow bus.

(6)

5

Going the limit on some slip of crabgrass,
vibrating to the everlasting motor,
a hundred yards, two hundred, above the ocean—
or once in New Orleans, when the ceiling fan
wrestled the moisture, and one pajama leg
hung out of reach, caught on a leather blade—
the generation bred to drink the ocean
in that all-possible after Repeal;
all girls then under twenty, and the boys
unearthly with the white blond hair of girls,
crawling the swimming pool's robin's-egg sky;
safe, out of reach. The fall warms vine and wire,
the ant's cool, amber, hyperthyroid eye,
grapes tanning on these tried entanglements.

6

Shake of the electric fan above our village;
oil truck, refrigerator, or just man,
nightly reloading of the village flesh—
there are worse things than marriage. Men find dates
wherever summer is out, the nights of the swallow
clashing in heat, storm-signal to stay home.
On Court Street, Dyer's Lane, School, Green and Main,
the moon-blanched blacktop fusses like a bosom,
dropping through shade-trees to the shadeless haven—
woman as white as ever. One only knows
her mother, sweatshirt gorged with tennis balls,
still air expiring from the lavish arc—
we too wore armor, strode riveted in cloth,
stiff as the broken clamshell labeled man.

(7)

7

They come, each year more gallant, playing chicken,
then braking to a standstill for a girl;
soft bullets hitting bottles, spars and gulls,
echo and ricochet across the bay—
hardy perennials. Kneedeep in the cowpond,
far from this cockfight, cattle stop and watch us,
then, having had their fill, go back to lapping
soiled water indistinguishable from heaven.
The cattle get through living, but to *live*:
Kokoschka at eighty, saying, "If you last,
you'll see your reputation die three times,
and even three cultures; young girls are always here."
Satyr and chick . . . two fray-winged dragonflies,
clinging to a thistle, too clean to mate.

8

The shore is pebbled with eroding brick,
seaweed in grizzled furrows—a surf-cast away,
a converted brickyard dormitory; higher,
the blacktop; higher yet, a fish-hawk's nest,
a bungalow, view-hung and staring, with wash
and picture-window—here, like offshoots that
have taken root. Grass shooting overnight,
sticks of dead rotten wood in drifts, the fish
with missing eyes, or heel-print on the belly,
or a gash in the back from a stray hook;
the lawns, the paths, the harbor—stitched with motors,
yawl-engine, outboard, power mower, plowing
the mangle and mash of the monotonous frontier,
bottles of dirt and lighted gasoline.

(8)

9

Two in the afternoon. The restlessness.
Greek Islands. Maine. I have counted the catalogue
of ships down half its length: the blistered canvas,
the metal bowsprits, once pricking up above
the Asian outworks like a wedge of geese,
the migrant yachtsmen, and the fleet in irons. . . .
The iron bell is rocking like a baby,
the high tide's turning on its back exhausted,
the colored, dreaming, silken spinnakers
shove through the patches in the island pine,
as if vegetating millennia of lizards fed
on fern and cropped the treetops . . . or nation of gazelles,
straw-chewers in the African siesta. . . .
I never thought scorn of things; struck fear in no man.

10

Up north here, in my own country, and free—
look on it with a jaundiced eye, you'll see
the manhood of the sallowing south, *noblesse
oblige* turned redneck, and the fellaheen;
yet sometimes the Nile is wet; life's lived as painted:
those couples, one in love and profit, swaying
their children and their slaves the height of children,
supple and gentle as giraffes or newts;
the waist still willowy, and the paint still fresh;
decorum without hardness; no harness on
the woman, and no armor on the husband,
the red clay Master with his feet of clay,
catwalking lightly through his conquests, leaving
one model, dynasties of faithless copies.

11

Both my legs hinged on the foreshortened bathtub,
small enough to have been a traveler's . . .
sun baking a bright fluff of balsam needles,
loose yellow swaths; and yet the scene confines;
sun falls on so many, many other things:
someone, Custer, leaping with his wind-gold scalplock,
a furlong or less from the old-style battle,
Sitting Bull's, who sent our hundreds under
in the Indian Summer—Oh that sunlit balsam,
this wizened window, the sea-haze of gauze blue
distance plighting the tree-lip of land to islands—
wives split between a playboy and a drudge.
Who can help us from our nothing to the all,
we aging downstream faster than a scepter can check?

12

Everyone now is crowding everyone
to put off leaving till the Indian Summer;
and why? Because the others will be gone—
we too, dull drops in the decamping mass,
one in a million buying solitude. . . .
We asked to linger on past fall in Eden;
there must be good in man. Life fears us. Death
keeps our respect by keeping at a distance—
death we've never outdistanced as the Apostle boasted . . .
stream of heady, terrified poured stone,
suburban highway, rural superhighway,
foot of skunkweed, masts of scrub . . . the rich poor. . . .
We are loved by being distant; love-longing
mists the windshield, soothes the eye with milk.

13

Mischievous fish-shapes without scale or eye
swimming your leaf-green teagown, maternal, autumnal,
swirling six inches past the three-inch heel,
collapsing on us like a parachute,
in a spate of controversial spatter . . . then
exhaustion. We hunger for the ancient fruit,
marriage with its naked artifice;
two practiced animals, close to widower
and widow, greedily bending forward
for the first handgrasp of vermilion leaves,
clinging like bloodclots to the smitten branch—
summer afield and whirling to the tropics,
to the dogdays and dustbowl—men, like ears of corn,
fibrous growths . . . green, sweet, golden, black.

14

Iced over soon; it's nothing; we're used to sickness;
too little perspiration in the bucket—
in the beginning, polio once a summer. Not that;
each day now the cork more sweetly leaves the bottle,
except a sudden falseness in the breath,
passive participation, dogged sloth,
angrily skirting greener ice, the naught
no longer asset or advantage. Sooner
or later, and the chalk wears out the smile,
this life too long for comfort and too brief
for perfection—Cro-Magnon, dinosaur—
the neverness of meeting nightly like surgeons'
apprentices studying their own skeletons,
old friends and mammoth flesh preserved in ice.

For Mary McCarthy

Your eight-inch, star-blue, softwood floorboard, your house
sawn for some deadport Revolutionary squire. . . .
A white horse doing small-point, flitching flies and smiling,
Dark Age luminary and Irish hothead,
the weathered yeoman loveliness of a duchess,
pale Diana, and rash to awkwardness. . . .
Whose will-shot arrows sing cleaner through the pelt?
You might say *will,* and not intelligence?
Others go on thinking it mind, mind, mind,
foundation on foundation, rococo stung,
stung repeatedly, by the battering ram's brass head of brass. . . .
I slip from wonder into bluster; you align
your lines more freely, ninety percent on target—
we can only meet in the bare air.

Searchings

1

I return then, but not to what I wanted—
a dull invulnerability to failure,
blood shooting through the fingertips of ivy,
hair and blown leaf bosom, the arrogant
tanned brunt behind her snow-starched shirt. . . . The white
bluffs rise above the old rock piers, now wrecked
beyond insuring by two hurricanes—
a boy would mount those scattered blocks, and leave
the sultry Sunday seaside crowds behind,
seeking landsend, his slight fishing rod,
duller and dimmer than a penciled eyebrow—
the boy, held over in the hollow classroom,
sanding down *RTSL*, his four initials, slashed
like a dirty word across the bare, blond desk.

2

I like the trees, because I can never be at their eye-level;
not even when the stiff sash of the New Hampshire farmhouse
slammed, as it always did, toward the morning's rise:
I dreaming I was sailing a very small sailboat,
with my mother one-eighth Jewish, and *her* mother two-eighths,
down the Hudson, twice as wide as it is, wide as the Mississippi,
sliding under the pylons of the George Washington Bridge,
childhood's twice-as-wide and twice-as-high,
lacework groins as tall as twenty trees—
landing in the coalsmoke and roses of
this river bar. . . . I am refreshed by the subway stop breath
of the black iron arbor. My knee-joints are melting—
O why was I born of woman? Never to reach their eye-level,
seeing the women's mouths while my date delays in the john.

3

There was no breakthrough, and no knowing—just
the thrilling, chilling silver of your laugh,
hysterical digging of the accursed spur,
Amazon, who saw me, cool and pop-eyed,
true, ageless, holding back her warwhoop—no chicken,
still game for swimming bare-ass with the boys.
The cur's chain rattles but the post stands fixed.
In dreams, you have fallen, pierced—unpayable
the bond for floating the impossible.
No hand will help us from the hole to China—
man, ninety-nine hundredths water, bred from water,
water fowl and water weed and whale,
water to water to water to water—how many
others have gone to this war, hope, death . . . dead drunk?

4

Almost innumerable the ties withheld;
nothing straitens you though, as with glassy eye
you weigh the frenetic goldfinch slung about
your lighthouse promontory, flights an inch
from combustion and the drab of ash—
a thousand summers . . . I would not count them; twenty
years back, your body was much the same as today,
dressed in a boy's bone-muscle, grit and curling lip . . .
even the treasonable bulge behind your fabric—
pile earth on earth, you cannot bury it!
Never revealed to me. I trust in your youth then;
youth keeps the foamrubber waterfall
from falling, makes the falling flesh stand firm
marble, pear-pointing to eternity.

(14)

Dream of the Fair Women

Those maidens' high waists, languorous steel and wedding cake,
fell, as waists would, white, white bust to white heel—
these once, the new wave; mostly they were many,
and would not let us speak. Girl-aunts, our sisters—
pace, pace: loss of innocence
never threw them; when we are impotent,
they are faithful. They'll keep us to the road
from chapel to graveyard. When they smooth the dead cheek,
it bleeds; the birch tree turns to a telephone pole,
knobs and tears and maidenhair—their plots
want no man's seeding; best of all they live.
Ten hours of this are like ten years back home,
when hurting others was as necessary as breathing,
hurting myself more necessary than breathing.

Five Dreams

1. *The Old Order*

Eyes shut, I hunt the vision through my eyelids:
first a bull's-head, Cretan black-bronze, high cheekbone
still brave with gilt—too military; I see
a girl's Bacchanalia with a wicker cow's-head;
she died of sleeping pills, but there's a tongue
of silverfoil still sticks in the wicker mouth;
now it's a horse's-head; this is better, it's nervous,
its eyes are string-shot like the bull's; but now,
my bestiary is interrupted: the man,
the beauty in checker trousers, strides the schoolroom;
he is eloquently angry, confiscates the ink-pots;
I wouldn't try this, but perhaps he did right—
a groom tends the black gate to the freestone graveyard—
old law and order that locked at the tap of a glove.

2. *Agamemnon: A Dream*

As I sleep, their saga comes out clarified:
why for three weeks mother toured the countryside,
buying up earthenware, big pots and urns,
Goliath's potsherds, such as the savage first
archaeologist broke on the first dig—our *own* art:
common the clay, kingly the workmanship.
As I sleep, streams of butane leak from my lighter;
for three weeks mother's foreign in-law kept carving
his chess-sets, leaf green, leaf red, as tall as urns,
modern Viking design for tribal Argos.
The King tripped on his pawns. . . . Suddenly, I see
father's eyes cross and bubble—a whiff of butane,
the muscle of a spitted ox bubbling by the urn. . . .
Can I call the police against my own family?

(16)

3. *The House in Argos*

O Christmas tree, how green thy branches—the features
could only be the most conventional,
the hardwood smiles, the Trojan rug's abstraction,
the firelight dancing to the Christmas candles,
the unusual offspring with his usual scowl,
naming all fifty states of Paradise,
with a red, blue, yellow pencil, while his mother,
seasick with marital unhappiness—
she has become the eye of heaven, she hates
her husband swimming like vagueness, like a porpoise,
on the imperial scarlet of the rug. . . .
His corpse in the candles is the fool's-gold lion,
his head is like the rich collection-plate,
singing, "O Christmas tree, how green thy branches . . ."

4. *The Next Dream*

"After my marriage, I found myself in constant
companionship with this almost stranger I found
neither agreeable, interesting, nor admirable,
though he was always kind and irresponsible.
The first years after our first child was born,
the daddy was out at sea; that helped, I could bask
in the rest and stimulation of my dreams,
but the courtship was too swift, the disembarkment
dangerously abrupt. I was animal,
healthy, easily tired; I adored luxury,
and should have been an extrovert; I usually
managed to make myself pretty comfortable. . . .
Well," she laughed, "we both were glad to dazzle.
A genius temperament should be handled with care."

5. *Onion Skin*

It's the fancy functional things love us best;
not mutely useful, or austerely useless,
they touch our bodies to assume a body.
My half-pound silver ticker had two bopped lids,
a sliver lever to be thumbnailed out
at *six,* and *six,* when all hands stopped, and time.
My watch ran to the clockmaker once too often.
Where's Grandfather's gold chain with the snake-head?
They go a-begging; without us, they are gone.
This typing paper pulped in Bucksport, Maine,
onion skin, only merchandised in Maine,
creased when I pulled the last sheet, and seemed to scream,
as if Fortuna bled in the white wood,
first felt the bloody gash that brought my life.

Through the Night

1

The pale green leaves cling white to the lit night:
this has been written, and eaten dead on carbons;
incendiaries strike no spark from this moonlight;
nothing less nutritive than the thirst at Harvard. . . .
Like the generation of leaves, the race of man;
their long hair, beads and jeans are early uniforms;
in this world, our world, deviation is prison.
I wake now, find myself this long alone,
stuck at eight-thirty, by the curb of a House,
waiting for my lift; it's the same for me
at fifty as at thirteen, my childish thirst
for the grown-ups in their open car and girls. . . .
She rides the hood and snuffs the smog of twilight:
"I want to live," she screams, "where I can see."

2

But the thick-skinned leaf flickers along its veins,
and shakes a little on the stiff, tense twig,
dancing its weekend jig in blood—Thank God;
for at the window of my house I looked,
I saw you walking with the simple ones,
in the twilight, in the evening, in the black, in the night;
not loud nor stubborn—and how earnestly,
I looked and found you lying on your bed;
you caught me and kissed me and stopped my rush,
your sinewy lips wide-eyed as the honeycomb,
your tongue as smooth as truth, your record-player
singing Gluck's *Orfeo,* the contralto's
"Where shall I go without Euridice?"
dying in our undergrowth, dense beyond reward.

3

The vague, dark new hallway, some darker rectangle:
the bathroom door, or a bedroom, someone else's;
saw of the wrong snoring, or, worse, the right—
each footstep a moral judgment, and the window
holds out its thin, black terminal disk of joy,
its blissfully withdrawing glimmer of immoral
retribution, as I lie awake basking,
trying to extend the dark, unspent minute,
as the window frame gradually burns green;
three panes still beam the polar blue of night,
as my backbone swims in the sperm of gladness,
as your figure emerges from your body,
we are two species, even from the inside—
a net trapped in the arms of another net.

4

Gradually greener in the window frame:
the old oil, unfamiliar here, alive
in a hundred eighteenth-century parks and landscapes—
Sir Joshua Reynolds might retouch each fault:
the cow-faced hound, the lonely, stalwart girl,
the scarlet general, more oaken than his oaks—
leaf, branch and trunk arranged as only money
and nobility, both somewhat outlaw here,
could render appropriate to the neighborhood:
one great window, one bright watching eye—
as achingly I awake to go the home-walk,
each pane, each windshield, familiar, unfamiliar,
each shingled, checkered window is sheer face,
the blindingly visible breasts freckle to brilliance.

5

Sloping, torn tarpaper on a wet roof,
on several roofs; here and there, a stray nail,
background of wrecked gingerbread Gothic,
a pop-art playground of psychedelic reds,
suburbia-proletarian. My judge was there:
cheeks of red brick powder, coarse horsetail hair,
Saint-Just, or anyone's nameless, mercantile
American ancestor of 1790—
head bowed, an elbow spiked on each sharp knee,
the cleansing guillotine peeping over his shoulder;
I climb the ladder, knowing my last words,
no matter how unjust, no longer matter,
the black marks of the night erased in blood—
wondering, "Why was it ever worth my while?"

6. *The Duc de Guise*

The grip gets puffy, and water wears the stones—
O to be always young among our friends,
as one of the countless peers who graced the world
with their murders and *joie de vivre,* made good
in a hundred aimless amorous bondages. . . .
Some great man, the Achilles, or the Guise,
warhawk and leader of the Holy League,
whose canopy and cell we saw at Blois,
just before he died, at the moment of orgasm,
his round eyes, hysterical and wistful,
a drugged bull's breathing, a cool, well-pastured brain,
his muscular, slacked-off stomach swelling
as if he were pregnant . . . before he sprang, his sword
unable to encircle the circle of his killers.

7

The green paint's always peeling from the prospect:
a man of eighty with the health of sixty,
strolling his lawn shaved smooth as a putting green—
this scene I could touch once, as I touch your hand,
our mirage future, keys jingling on the sky's
blue smoke-ring. How many enthusiasts are gone;
their bound legs march, the impudent standards
part the dust of the field, the fog of battle;
and the heart's moisture goes up like a summer drought.
We are firemen smashing holes in our own house.
We will each breath, and make our peace with war,
yearning to swoop with the swallow's brute joy,
indestructible as mercy—the round green weed
slipping free from the disappointment of the flower.

The Muse

1. *Nantucket: 1935*

(TO FRANK PARKER)

She never married, because she loved to talk,
"You watch the waves *woll* and *woll* and *woll* and *woll*,"
she lisped, and that was how we picked Nantucket.
I watched but little, though I tried the surf,
hung dead on its moment of infinity,
corked between water, sky and gravel, smothered,
smitten loose from volition. When I breathe now,
I hear that distant pant of gulls in my chest,
but death then was our classmate killed skidding on
a Vineyard sand-swerve—a first death, and its image:
your seascape of Moses breaking the Ten Commandments
against a mount of saltgrass, dune and surf,
repainted, then repainted, till the colors browned
to a whirl of mud in the hand of Michelangelo.

2. *The Muses of George Grosz*

Berlin in the twenties bore the bell away,
elsewhere the music crept, the paintings stank;
the iron hand of politics had clenched—
our artists too, they rush to break the windows,
as if we'd limped past Germany at last.
Grosz men are one man, Marshal von Hindenburg,
from crib to Methuselah, paying gold for Venus;
none ever strip—Grosz women always shed:
girls one might meet at Modern Language Annuals,
pushing retirement, weighing more than men;
and once the least were good for the all-night game—
if one could swing the old sows by their tits:
the receding hairlines of those nettled cunts
severed like scalplocks by the stroke of a brush.

(23)

Randall Jarrell: 1914–1965

1

Sixty, seventy, eighty: I see you mellow,
unchanging cricket, whistling down the grass-fires;
the same hair, snow-shocked, and wrist for tennis; now doubles,
not singles. . . . Who dares bridge that deadfall, sit
with you, watch the ivy turn, a wash of blood
on the infirmary wall, a fifth-act autumn,
see the years wrinkling up the reservoir?
Students waiting for Europe and spring term to end,
we saw below us, golden, small, stockstill,
cornfields and polo field, the feudal campus airdrome,
its Georgian Trust; behind, above us, castle,
towers, dorms, fieldhouse, bishop's house and chapel—
Randall, the same fall splinters on the windshield,
the same apples wizen on the whiplash bough.

2

Grizzling up the embers of our onetime life,
our first intoxicating disenchantments,
dipping our hands once, twice, in the same river,
entrained for college on the Ohio local;
the scene shifts, middle distance, back and foreground,
things changing position like chessmen on a wheel,
drawn by a water buffalo, perhaps
blue with true space before the dawn of days—
then the night of the caged squirrel on its wheel:
lights, eyes, peering at you from the overpass;
black-gloved, black-coated, you plod out stubbornly,
as if asleep, Child Randall, as if in chainstep,
meeting the cars, and approving; with harsh
luminosity grasping at the blank coin of the tunnel.

Munich, 1938

Hitler, Mussolini, Daladier, Chamberlain:
that historic confrontation of the great—
firm on one thing, they were against the war;
each won there, by shoving the war ahead twelve months.
Is it worse to choke on the vomit of cowardice,
or blow the world up on a point of honor? . . .
John Crowe Ransom at Kenyon College, Gambier, Ohio,
looking at primitive African art on loan:
gleam-bottomed naked warriors of oiled brown wood,
makeshift tin straws in their hands for spears;
far from the bearded, armored, all-profile hoplite
on the Greek vase; not distant maybe in their gods—
John saying, "Well, they may not have been good neighbors,
but they never troubled the rest of the world."

August 22, 1968

October and November

1. Che Guevara

Week of Che Guevara, hunted, hurt,
held prisoner one lost day, then gangstered down
for gold, for justice—violence cracking on violence,
rock on rock, the corpse of the last armed prophet
laid out on a sink in a shed, displayed by flashlight—
as the leaves light up, still green, this afternoon,
and burn to frittered reds; as the oak, branch-lopped
to go on living, swells with goiters like a fruit-tree,
as the sides of the high white stone buildings over-
shadow the poor, too new for the new world,
Manhattan, where our clasped, illicit hands
pulse, stop the bloodstream as if it hit rock. . . .
Rest for the outlaw . . . kings once hid in oaks,
with prices on their heads, and watched for game.

2. Caracas

Through another of our cities without a center, as hideous
as Los Angeles, and with as many cars
per head, and past the 20-foot neon sign
for *Coppertone* on a church, past the population
earning $700 per capita
in jerry skyscraper living-slabs, and on to the White House
of El Presidente Leoni, his small men with 18-
inch repeating pistols, firing 45 bullets a minute,
the two armed guards petrified beside us, while we had champagne,
and someone bugging the President: "Where are the girls?"
And the enclosed leader, quite a fellow, saying,
"I don't know where yours are, but I know where to find mine." . . .
This house, this pioneer democracy, built
on foundations, not of rock, but blood as hard as rock.

3. *The March*

(FOR DWIGHT MACDONALD)
Under the too white marmoreal Lincoln Memorial,
the too tall marmoreal Washington Obelisk,
gazing into the too long reflecting pool,
the reddish trees, the withering autumn sky,
the remorseless, amplified harangues for peace—
lovely to lock arms, to march absurdly locked
(unlocking to keep my wet glasses from slipping)
to see the cigarette match quaking in my fingers,
then to step off like green Union Army recruits
for the first Bull Run, sped by photographers,
the notables, the girls . . . fear, glory, chaos, rout . . .
our green army staggered out on the miles-long green fields,
met by the other army, the Martian, the ape, the hero,
his new-fangled rifle, his green new steel helmet.

4. *The March*

Where two or three were heaped together, or fifty,
mostly white-haired, or bald, or women . . . sadly
unfit to follow their dream, I sat in the sunset
shade of their Bastille, the Pentagon,
nursing leg- and arch-cramps, my cowardly,
foolhardy heart; and heard, alas, more speeches,
though the words took heart now to show how weak
we were, and right. An MP sergeant kept
repeating, "March slowly through them. Don't even brush
anyone sitting down." They tiptoed through us
in single file, and then their second wave
trampled us flat and back. Health to those who held,
health to the green steel head . . . to the kind hands
that helped me stagger to my feet, and flee.

5. *Charles Russell Lowell: 1835–1864*

Hard to exhume him from the other Union martyrs;
though common now, his long-short, crisping hair,
his green mustache, the manly, foppish coat—
more and more often he turns up as a student:
twelves horses killed under him—a nabob cousin
bred, then shipped their replacements. He had, *gave* . . . everything
at Cedar Creek—his men dismounted, firing
repeating carbines; heading two vicious charges,
the slug collapsing his bad, tubercular lung:
fainting, bleeding, loss of voice above a whisper;
Phil Sheridan—any captain since Joshua—shouting:
"I'll sleep in the enemy camp tonight, or hell. . . ."
Charles had himself strapped to the saddle . . . bound to death,
his cavalry that scorned the earth it trod on.

6. *Caracas*

With words handled like the new grass writhing, rippling
in an urban brook, greens washed to double greenness—
one could get through life, though mute, with courage
and a merciful heart—two things, and a third thing:
humor . . . as the turned-out squatter clings
with amused bravery that takes the form of mercy
to the Old Square in Caracas, his shaky, one-man hovel,
the spoiled baroque cathedral from the age of Drake.   [Common—
The church has hay in its courtyard; householders own the
conservatives reduced to conservation:
green things, the well, the school, the writhing grass;
the communist committed to his commune,
artist and office-holder to a claque of less
than fifty souls . . . to each his venomous in-group.

(28)

Autumn in the Abstract

1. *Alba*

The building's color is fresh unfinished wood of
an old penny postcard; thirty stories seem hundreds,
with miniature view-windows that gleam like cells;
on a wafer balcony, too thin for human sitters,
hangs a crimson blazer, a replica
of the one I wear, but this is hollow, blows
to the fall air, shines with a Harvard shield. . . .
Eve and Adam, adventuring from the ache
of the first sleep, met forms less primitive
and honest, when they gazed on the stone-ax
and Hawaiian fig-leaf hanging from their fig-tree. . . .
Nothing more established, pure and lonely,
than the early Sunday morning in New York—
the sun on high burning, and most cars dead.

2. *In Sickness*

The desultory, profitable fall
lies like a mustard plaster on our backs,
determines us to labor, steal and pay. . . .
If I look for the unbelievably beautiful
in a city, it's mostly women in their war-paint—
the brave stands buckled to his scourge of armor,
the chemist smiles etherealized in his turret.
Sometimes, my mind is a rocked and dangerous bell,
I climb the spiral steps to my own music;
a friend drops in the pit, then no one stirs.
Pavlov's dogs, when tortured, turned neurotics;
the cure: rest, exercise, fresh air and meals.
When we are brainwashed, we are read the book. . . .
In sickness, the mind and body make a marriage.

3. Deutschland über Alles

Hitler, though we laugh, gave them the start,
the step forward, one had to give them that:
the Duce's, "Once they start marching, they'll never stop."
Joy in the introversion of loneliness,
the silver reichsmark quivering to the heel,
the knights corrupted by their purity,
made wilder by the wildness of the woodcut—
his eyes were glowing coals, the world turned dark,
the horde, on stopwatch, asked for earth and water,
settled for *lebensraum,* then *lebensraum:*
spaces, a space, the night astride the eyetooth.
Who will contest the conqueror his dirt,
spaces enough to bury what they left,
the six million Jews gassed in the space to breathe?

4. End of the Saga

"Even if they will murder the whole world,
we'll hit them so hard, they'll never tell the story."
Kriemhild was shouting, "If they get to the air,
and cool their coats of mail, we are all lost."
Then the great hall was fired; we saw them kneel
beside their corpses, and drink the flowing blood—
unaccustomed to such drink, they thought it good,
in the great heat, it tasted cooler than wine.
They tried to lift their brothers from the fire,
they found them too hot to hold, and let them drop.
"O why are we so wet with our lifeblood?"
they asked. "Our bones are broken, not our hearts. . . ."
The king is laughing, all his men are killed,
he is shaken by the news, as well he might be.

Symbols

1. *The Well*

The stones of the well were sullenly unhewn,
none could deny their leechlike will to stay—
no dwelling near and four square miles of flatness,
pale grass diversified by wounds of sand,
the grass as hard as rock and squeezed by winter,
each well-stone rounded as an ostrich egg,
strange for unfinished stone. It seemed a kind
of dead chimney. The halting trespasser
was free to pitch the bucket, drinking cup
and funnel down the well—his neighbor's bucket
through bottomless, thin black hoops of standing water,
and plenty of elbowroom for scuttled gear;
room to reach the bottom, unnoticed, uncrushed. . . .
It's not the crowds, but crowding kills the soul.

2. *Hell*

"Circles of Dante—and in that dirt-roofed cave,
each family had marked off its yard of space;
no light except their coal fires laid in buckets,
no draft of air except their smoke, no water,
no hole to hide the excrement. I walked on,
afraid of stumbling on the helpless bodies,
afraid of circling. I soon forgot the Fascist
or German deserters I was hunting—screaming
children, old men, old women, coughing and groaning.
Then hit my head on the low dirt, and reached out
to keep from falling or hurting anyone;
and what I touched was not the filthy floor:
a woman's hand returning my quick grasp,
her finger tracing the lifeline on my palm."

(31)

3. *Rats*

A friend of that day, the Black Muslim
on our masons' gang at the Danbury Jail,
held his hand over the postcard Connecticut
landscape, scarred by us and a few mean human houses,
saying, "Only man is miserable."
He was wrong though, he forgot the rats. A pair
in an enclosure kills the rest, then breeds a clan.
Stranger rats with their wrong clan-smell stumble
on the clan, are run squeaking with tails and backs split open
up trees and fences—to die of nervous shock.
Someone rigged the enclosure with electric levers
that could give the rats an orgasm. Soon the rats learned
to press the levers, did nothing else—still on the trip,
they died of starvation in a litter of food.

4. *In the Cage*

The lifers file into the hall,
according to their houses—twos
of laundered denim. On the wall
a colored fairy tinkles blues
and titters by the balustrade;
canaries sing the bars, and scream.
We come from tunnels where the spade
pickax and hod for plaster steam
in mud and insulation. Here
the Bible-twisting Israelite
fasts for his Harlem. It is night,
and it is vanity; the age
numbs the failed nerve to service. Fear,
the yellow chirper, beaks its cage.

Winter 1944 [from *Lord Weary's Castle*]

5. *The River God*

The Aztecs gave the human sacrifice
credit-cards, dames, the usual pork of kings;
after a year, the king was cooled with palm-slash;
none ever detected he had lost his heart—
gods, and the sun was succored by their blood . . .
Mao had to find ways to economize on lepers;
each family had a leper, fed it like a pig;
Mao announced the people's plan for leprosy,
the lepers came bounding from the filth of hiding,
more lepers than Jordan or Tigris ever washed,
from Naaman to the popular cures of Christ . . .
Then doped like kings, the boatride colorful,
launched on the Yangtze with a thousand flowers—
the river god caught them in his arms when they drowned.

6. *The Leak*

We must have seven-league boots to cross these tiles;
drops strike with the tock of the town clock,
then more rapidly than the second hand;
it's like industry's dogged, clogged pollution—
a soaked roll of tissue, scored like a Moslem tile,
your saturated, crested bathmat, wadded
to a sprinkling pipe and alchemized to water;
in the basin, gold ringlets of your pubic hair. . . .
I hear our water torture, murmur of rivers:
Let us cross over the river and rest under the trees. . . .
We open the window, and there is no view,
no green meadow pointing to *the* green meadow,
to dogs, to deer, Diana in her war-skirt. . . .
Heaven must be paved with terra-cotta tile.

(33)

For Aunt Sarah

You never had the constitution to quarrel:
poised, warm and cool, distrusting beards and greatness,
yet infinitely kind—in short a lady,
still reaching past the turn of the century
for your youth in that solid golden age, when means
needed only to follow the golden mean
to guide and enjoy the world; when business captains
and their crews of statesmen willingly gave up
health, wealth and pleasure for the stones of office,
guided by their only fiction, God.
But this new age? "They have no fun," you say. . . .
We've quarreled lightly almost fifty years,
Dear, long enough to know how high our pulse beats, while the
wish to stand in our shoes before we've left them.   [young

The Heavenly Rain

Man is the root of everything he builds;
no nature, except the human, loves New York—
the clerk won't prove Aseity's existence
by bussing from helpless cause to helpless cause. . . .
The rain falls down from heaven, though heaven keeps
her noble distance, Dancer, seen not heard.
The rain falls down, the soil swims up to breathe,
the squatter sumac, shafted in cement,
flirts its wet leaves to heaven like the Firebird.
Two girls clasp hands in a clamshell courtyard to watch
the weed of the sumac aging visibly;
the girls age not, are always young as last week,
wish all rains one rain—this, that will not wash
the fallen leaf, turned scarlet, back to green.

Charles River

1

The sycamores throw shadows on the Charles,
while the fagged insect splinters to rejoin
the infinite, now casting its loose leaf
on the short-skirted girl and long-haired escort,
and the black stream curves, as if it led a lover—
not so our blood: in workaday times,
one takes cold comfort in its variations,
its endless handspring round the single I,
the pounding and pumping of overfevered zeal;
but for a week our blood has pointed elsewhere:
it brings us here tonight, and ties our hands—
if we leaned forward, and should dip a finger
into this river's momentary black flow,
the infinite small stars would break like fish.

2

The circuit of those snow-topped rural roads, eight miles
to ten, might easily have been the world's
top, round the pole, when I trailed on spreading skis
my guide, his unerring legs ten inches thick in wool,
and pinched my earlobes lest they turn to snowdrops—
hard knocks to school a lifetime; yet I went on swiping
small things. That knife, snow-yellow with eleven blades,
where is it now? It will outlast us all,
though flawed already when I picked it up. . . .
And now, the big town river, once hard and dead as its highways,
rolls blackly into country river, root-banks, live ice,
a live muskrat muddying the moonlight. You trail me,
Woman, so small, if one could trust the appearance,
I might be in trouble with the law.

3

My father's letter to your father, saying
tersely and much too stiffly that he knew
you'd been going to my college rooms alone—
I can still almost crackle that slight note in my hand.
I see your outraged father; you, his outraged daughter;
myself brooding in fire and a dark quiet
on the abandoned steps of the Harvard Fieldhouse,
calming my hot nerves and enflaming my mind's
nomad quicksilver by saying *Lycidas*—
Then punctiliously handing the letter to my father.
I knocked him down. He half-reclined on the carpet;
Mother called from the top of the carpeted stairs—
our glass door locking behind me, no cover; you
idling in your station wagon, no retreat.

4

If the clock had stopped in 1936
for them, or again in '50 and '54—
they are not dead, and not until death parts us,
will I stop sucking my blood from their hurt.
They say, "I had my life when I was young."
They must have . . . dying young in middle-age;
yet often the old grow still more beautiful,
watering out the hours, biting back their tears,
as the white of the moon streams in on them unshaded;
and women too, the tanning rose, their ebb,
neither a medical, nor agricultural problem.
I struck my father; later my apology
hardly scratched the surface of his invisible
coronary . . . never to be effaced.

5

Longer ago than we had lived till then,
before the *Anschluss,* the thirty or forty million
war-dead . . . but who knows now offhand how many?
I tasted first love gazing through your narrow
bay window at the hideous concrete dome
of M.I.T., the last blanched, hectic glow
sunset-blackened on the bay of the Esplanade:
an imperial shrine in a landscape by Claude Lorrain,
an artist out of fashion, like Nero, his Empire
of heaven-vaulting aqueducts, baths, arches,
roads, legions, plowshares beaten down to swords,
the blood of the spirit lost in veins of brickdust—
Christ also, our only king without a sword,
turning the word forgiveness to a sword.

6

No stars worth noticing; the lights of man
lunge road and sky; and life is wild here: straw
puts teeth in the shore strip; the water smells and lives.
We walk our tightrope, this embankment, jewed—
no, yankeed—by the highways down to a grassy lip. . . .
Once—you weren't born then—an iron railing,
charmless and dignified, policed this walk;
it matched the times, and had an esplanade,
stamping down grass and growth with square stone shoes;
the Charles itself, half ink, half liquid coaldust,
testified to the health of industry—
wrong times, an evil dispensation; yet who
can hope to enter heaven with clean hands?
A groan went up when the iron railing crashed.

7

No outward and visible sign, the sleep unbroken,
except when winds thrust through the smooth stone cube,
our bedroom, putty-gray and putty-cool. . . .
A car or two, then none; or always none.
Roads on three levels parallel the river,
roads pace the river in a losing struggle,
forces of nature trying to breathe beneath
the jacket of lava. We lie parallel,
parallel to the river, parallel
to six roads—unmoving and awake,
awake and naked, like a line of Greeks
facing a second line of Greeks—like them,
willing to enter the battle, and not come out . . .
morning's lawful traffic . . . the unbroken snore.

My Grandfather

A nose flat-bent, not hawk, cheeks razored sand—
Velásquez' self-portrait is James MacDonald,
Jim to grandfather, MacDonald to the children,
though always *Mr.* in our vocative.
Having one's farmer then was like owning a car.
He sits on his lawn waiting a lift to the Old Men's Home;
saying? Here even the painter's speaking likeness ends;
nor could he paint my grandfather. I've overtaken
most of the elders of my youth, not this one,
yet I begin to know why he stood the frost
so many weekends with his little grandson
sawing up his trees for a penny a log—
Old Cato, ten years to live, preferring this squander
to his halcyon Roman credits from the Boom.

Names

1. Sir Thomas More

Hans Holbein's More, my friend since World War II,
the gold chain of *S's,* the golden rose,
the plush cap, the brow's damp feathertips of hair,
the slate eyes' stern, facetious twinkle, ready
to turn from executioner to martyr—
or saunter with the great King's bluff arm on his neck,
feeling that friend-slaying, terror-ridden heart
beating under the fat of Aretino—
some hanger-on saying, "How the King must love you!"
And Thomas, "If it were a question of my head,
or losing his meanest village in France . . ." Or standing
below the scaffold and the two-edged sword—
"Friend, help me up," he said, "when I come down,
my head and body will shift for themselves."

2. Marcus Cato the Younger

Cato too, a boy still, at Sulla's villa, the tombs,
saw people come in as men, and leave as heads.
"Why hasn't someone killed him?" he asked. They answered,
"Men fear Sulla even more than they hate him."
"Give me a sword." Thereafter his word was a sword;
tasting Plato and wine all night with friends,
gambling his life in the Forum, stoned like Paul,
he went on speaking while the soldiers saved their State,
saved Caesar. . . . At the last cast of his lost cause,
he bloodied his hand on a slave who hid his sword;
he fell in a small sleep, then heard the small birds chirping.
His bruised hand struck. When they tried to put back his bowels,
he tore them with his own hands. . . . He's where he would be:
a Roman who died, perhaps, for Rome.

3. Joinville and Louis IX

"Given my pilgrim's scarf and staff, I left
the village of Joinville on foot, barefoot, in my shirt,
never turning my eyes for fear my heart would melt
at leaving my mortgaged castle, my two fair children—
a Crusader? Some of us lived, and many ransomed
bishops, nobles and Brothers of the King
strolled free in Acre, and begged the King to sail home,
and desert the meaner folk. Sore of heart then,
I went to a barred window, and passed my arms through the bars
of the window, and someone came, and leant on my shoulders,
and placed his two hands on my head. 'Philip of Nemours,'
I screamed, 'leave me in peace!' The hands fell by chance,
and I knew the King by the emerald on his hand:
'If I should leave Jerusalem, who will remain?'"

4. Alexander

His sweet moist eye missed nothing—the vague guerrilla,
untested ground, the untested tactic, the hell-fire drive,
the pundit knotting his net of dialectic—
his phalanxes kept oiled ten years for the crux of battle,
his engines engineered to the fall of Tyre—
Achilles . . . but in Aristotle's corrected copy—
health burning like the dewdrop on that flesh
hit in a hundred calculated sallies,
to give the Persians the cup of love, his brothers—
the wine-bowl of the Macedonian drinking bout . . .
drinking out of friendship, then meeting Medius,
then drinking, then bathing, then sleeping, then meeting Medius,
then drinking, then bathing . . . dead at thirty-two—
in this life only is our hope in Christ.

5. *Napoleon*

Boston's used bookshops, holdovers from London, are gone;
hard even now to fathom why I spent
my vacations lugging home the third-hand *Lives*—
shaking the dust from that stationery stock:
myopic lithograph, and gilt-edged pulp
on a man—not bloodthirsty, not sparing of blood;
with the ways and means to manage everything;
his iron hand, no soft appendage to his brain,
fell with the mortal quickness of his lust,
uprooting races, kingdoms, Jacobins—
the price was paltry . . . three million soldiers dead,
grand opera fixed like morphine in their veins.
Dare I say, he had no moral center?
All gone like the smoke of his own artillery?

6. *Waterloo*

Hung thunderclouded over the mantel of our summer
cottage by the owners, Miss Barnard or Mrs. Curtis:
a sad engraving, half life-scale, removed now, and no doubt
wrecked as too imperial and raw for our stomachs:
Waterloo, Waterloo! You could choose sides then:
the French uniforms, a blue-black, came out black,
the British Redcoats gray; those running were French—
one, an aide-de-camp, Napoleon's clearly, wore
a waterfall of overstated braid,
there sabered, dying, his standard wrenched from weak hands
by his killer, a helmeted, fog-gray dragoon,
the true Britannia, the rib of oak—
six centuries, this field of their encounter,
La Gloire changing to *sauve qui peut* and *merde.*

Harvard

1

Beauty-sleep for the writer, and the beauty,
both fighting off muscular cramps, the same fatigue.
Lying in bed, letting the bright, white morning
rise to mid-heaven through a gag of snow,
through high school, through college, through the last vacation—
I've slept so late here, snow has stubbled my throat;
students in their hundreds rise from the beehive,
swarm-mates; they have clocks and instincts, make
classes. In the high sky, a parochial school,
the top floors looking like the Place des Vosges—
a silk stocking, blown thin as smog, coils in a twig-fork,
dangling a wire coathanger, rapier-bright—
a long shot for a hard cold day . . . wind lifting
the stocking like the lecherous, lost leg.

2

Each hour the stocking thins, the hanger dulls;
cold makes the thin green copper cupola
greener over the defoliated playground;
clouds lie in cotton wads on the Dutch sky,
death to the superhuman, worse for the human.
My mind can't hold the focus for a minute.
A sentence? A paragraph? The best tale
stales to homework. Flash-visions; as if I saw
the dark of the moon on the white of my eye;
and now, her Absent-present . . . black fishnet legs,
curve of the hourglass standing by the shower,
shut, verbalizing lips, her finger pointing;
no clean slate! And who will sit out the sermon?
The clean blade is too sharp, the old poisons.

3

The gluttony of eating out alone
here in Cambridge, where anyone can be no one,
and the people we'd flee at dinner parties change
to the mysterious, the beautiful . . .
on display on my small table, overwhite,
overobserved, ignored . . . the moment tries
my soul grown seasick on cold solitude—
the swimmer has chickened short of Labrador;
yet everyone who is seated is a lay,
or Paul Claudel. He's near me now, declaiming:
"L'Académie Groton, eh, c'est une école admirable,"
soaring from hobbled English to a basic French,
a vocabulary poorer than Racine's,
no word unknown, no syntax understood.

4

Inching along the bayfront on the icepools,
sea and shipping cut out by the banks of cars,
and our relationship advancing or
declining to private jokes, and chaff and lust. . . .
Our leeway came so seldom, fell so short,
overwatched by some artist's skylight in the city,
or some suburban frame-house basement window,
angular, night-bluish, blear-eyed, spinsterish—
still this is something, something we can both
take hold of willingly, go smash on, if we will:
all flesh is grass, and like the flower in the field;
no! lips, breasts, eyes, hands, lips, hair;
as the overworked central heating bangs the frame,
as a milkhorse, time gone, would crash the morning milkcan.

Alcohol

1

Brown hours, they stream like water off the back.
One wants to top the crowns of the tallest flowers
with the blade of the hand, sweep, sweep and down sweep,
running in bullhorns down the garden path,
seeing left, right and wrong are in the wind. . . .
Harder to be the audience than the stage,
live in the small and right Horatian suburb:
the lawn is skinned, tense the wife, the mighty torrent
lost in the melancholy stream of traffic.
I would stop and sun, but my lips keep twitching:
"I suffer more for myself than for you.
I burn the bottle's universal sun,
the spineless vermin slink stinking from the woodwork;
suddenly, no disinclination to murder."

2

Pale ale, molar drain . . . I face the men's room mirror,
walrus mustaches, or antlers, two bad tusks.
But I am clean-shaven, I love the sheer of shaving—
make love, not war, or girls. Who will buy that?
I am a worshipper of myth and monster:
faces hairy as coal-drift shredded wheat,
soaks beheaded by a bronze and hairless stripling,
his bare flesh comely as the new-mown lawn.
Comb never touched the hair of John the Baptist;
or was it Samson? Or was it alcohol
never passed his lips? Moses, who saw the Mountain
soar past timberline to *petrus mortis?*
In the Gardens of Allah, man still wears the beard,
the women are undressed, accepting love.

3

Nature might do her thing for us; so they swore,
with peeled staff, imbecility and psalter
scrounging Northumberland for the infinite;
camping on a shorefront where the dusk seal
nightly dog-paddles on the hawk for fish,
whiskering giddy the harbor, a black blanket
patched up with splotches of the sky, sky-sky,
bluebird and blackbird blending into black;
where the Brook Trout dolphins by the housepiles,
grows common by mid-vacation as hamburger,
its fish-translucence cooked to the white of an egg;
or see the young yachts, half your income, come
about at your bulwark—they are no longer than your car;
you, no larger than the shoe you fit.

In the Forties

1

The back-look? Green logs sizzled on the fire-dogs,
painted scarlet like British Redcoats. June
steamed up in greenness; in the sopping trees
the green frog whistled to the greener sigh
of the new leaf—jay and catbird afoot,
head cocked for earthworms in the sidewalk puddles—
and you, dear, coming to our house, where words
were seldom passed except in public. . . . Hot
from toiling up the Portland Wagon Road,
we saw the burial ground of the Abenaki,
French converts, called the Praying Niggers, though
this helped them little with the English, who
scalped, killed and burned brave, squaw and child; then held
this field . . . as later we, newcomers, free.

2

The heron warped its neck, a broken pick,
to study its reflection in the glare
of the lily pads bright as mica, swarming
with plant-lice in the wood-blood water.
I held you, while your ballet glasses held
the heron twisted by a fist of alder,
your figure's synonym—a chest so thin then,
your ribs stood out like bars. . . . Great men had dwelt here,
lords of their self-inflicted desiccation,
roaming for passage through the virgin forest,
stalked by a far more greenly brutal quarry
down the warpaths to wives and twenty children—
many of them, too many, love, to count . . .
born to fill up the graveyards . . . thick as sticks.

3

Even in August, it turned autumn . . . all
the public lake could harbor. No sound; no talk;
the dead match nicked the water and expired,
a target-circle on inverted sky,
nature's mirror . . . just a little cold!
Our day was cold and short, love, and its sun,
numb as the red carp, twenty inches long,
panting, a weak old dog, below a smashed
oar floating from a metal dock. The fish
is fungus; we too wear a larger face.
I rowed for the reflection, but it slid
between my fingers and grounded. . . . There the squirrels,
conservatives and vegetarians,
hold their roots and freehold, love, unsliding.

The Literary Life, a Scrapbook

My photo: I before I was I, or a book;
inch-worm! A cheekbone gumballs out my cheek;
too much live hair. My wife caught in that eye blazes,
an egg would boil in the tension of that hand;
the dragging shoestrings write my name in the dust. . . .
I rest on a tree, and try to sharpen bromides
to serve the great, the great God, the New Critic,
who loves the writing better than we ourselves. . . .
In those days, if I pressed an ear to the earth,
I heard the bass growl of Hiroshima. No!
In the *Scrapbook,* it's the old who die classics:
one foot in the grave, and two in his books—that's living!
Who wouldn't rather be his indexed correspondents
than the boy Keats spitting out blood for time to bleed?

Sleep

1

Four windows, five feet tall, soar up like windows,
rinsing their stained-glass angels in the void,
interminably alert the four-hour stay till morning:
a watery dearth, made plain, and made to last
by a light or two hung on a telephone pole;
ashcan and alley, the makeshift rooming-house,
clawed loose from packing crates, and painted gray,
frozen interminably to this four-hour verge. . . .
Heaven? Time stops here too—Flesh of my Flesh,
elastic past the mind's agility,
hair coiled back on guard like the spring of a watch,
legs showing pale as wooden matches, lit
by four streak windows of the uncreating dawn,
not night or day, here stealing a brief life from both.

2

Six straight hours to teach on less than three hours' sleep—
I know I'll be smitten by the hand of my cells,
my gray hairs will not go down to the grave in peace. . . .
I get to know myself, old bluff and bruiser,
who cannot stand up to the final round. . . .
To enjoy the avarice of loneliness,
sleep the hour hand round the clock, stay home,
lie like a hound, on bounds for chasing a hound,
roped short in a spare corner, nose on paws,
one eyelid raised to guard the bowl of water;
panting, "Better to die, than hate or fear,
better die twice than make ourselves feared or hated—
no, happier to live in a land without history;
where the bad-liver lives longer than the law."

3

An aquamarine bottle twinkles on a pane;
outside, a one-story factory with a spook chimney,
built in the age of trains and Robert Fulton,
condemned by law and Harvard, still alive.
A first tiger cat stationed on the record-player
spies on a second reaching from its carton-
dollhouse to bat a brass ball on a string;
the tree, untinseled, asymmetrical,
shoves up askewly blessing a small sprawl
of sealed, blank-papered Christmas packages;
your girl, she's nine still, comes wisely, inopportunely
reappearing—you standing up on your bed
in your Emily Dickinson nightgown, purely marveling
whether to be sensible or drown.

Blizzard in Cambridge

Risen from the blindness of teaching to bright snow,
and everything mechanical stopped dead:
taxis thumbs-down on fares, tires burning the ice;
wet eye, iced eyelash, spring-wear; subways held,
too jammed and late to wait for passengers;
to snow-trekking the mile from subway end to airport,
to all-flights-canceled, to the queues congealed
to telephones out of order, to the groping buses,
to rich, stranded New Yorkers staring with the wild, mild eyes
of steers at the foreign subway—then the train home,
rolling with stately scorn: an hour in Providence,
another in New Haven—in darkness seeing
white arsenic numbers on the tail of a downed plane,
the smokestacks of abandoned fieldguns burning skyward.

Christmas and New Year

1. Snake

One of God's creatures, just as much as you,
or God; what other bends its back in crooks
and curves so gracefully, or yields a point;
brews a more scalding venom from cooler blood;
or flings its spine-string noosed about their throats:
hysterical bird, wild pig, or screaming rabbit?
Often I see it sunning on bright, brisk days,
when the heat has ebbed from its beloved rocks;
it is seamless, scaled-down to its integrity,
coiled for indiscriminate malevolence.
Lately, its hubris pushed it past man's patience;
stoned, flesh-chipped, it holds its hole now, sentenced
to hibernate fifty years. . . . It will thaw, then kill—
my little lamb in wolfskin, whip of wisdom.

2. Christmas Tree

Twenty or more big cloth roses, rose-color or scarlet,
coil in the branches—a winning combination
for you, who have gathered them eight years or more:
bosom-blossoms from Caribbean steambath forests,
changeless, though changed from tree to tree, unchanged
and transplants—like you, I think: twenty small birds or more,
nipping the needles; a quail, a golden warbler. . . .
And the others? Run of the mill; except for those minnowy
green things, no known species, made of woven straw:
little laundry hampers and steamer trunks for the elves.
A fine thing, built with love; though too unconventional
for our child to buy. . . . Who can bear the modesty
and righteousness of the woman's ego stripped naked:
"Because I lacked ambition, men thought me mad"?

3. *The Dialogue*

Old campaigner, I must surrender something,
tenting tonight and tenting under arms,
not talking for victory but survival—
only when we were assaulted were we Mongols,
meaning—let's forget the breakage—words.
You had just provocation: in the cool hour,
the monk and libertine kept swapping masks,
rough spice of cavalier and puritan.
How could we nurse one family glass of Bourbon
through two half hours of television news,
through politics of the day, and the evening news?
Unbuttoned, heaven pumped in heartbeats to my forehead,
the cherry rolling in the rosecolored glass of spirits . . .
How could two spirits get to bed on that?

4. *Playing Ball with the Critic*
(FOR RICHARD BLACKMUR)

We're trained to practice to kick the ball
to the police, and smile and even like it;
they too like it, smile and kick the ball;
the hurt blue muscles work like testicles;
where else can we learn to duck and block the knock?
"Is it a form of a force, or sentiment of a form?
His logic lacerates his vision, vision turns
his logic to zealotry," or, "In his first, best, book,
no poem offers a logical evaluation."—
still, it's a privilege to earn the bullring.
Jealousy seldom comes from the sublime;
it is a passage in our cups at dinner,
the pretty girl, though a critic and our wife,
sends us home kicking each bleeding leaf of the weeds.

5. *George H. and George E. Lewes*

A lady in bonnet, brow clearer than the Virgin,
the profile of a white rhinoceros—
but as for living, they left it to the servants,
and neither ever wished a second youth,
and neither wished to garden, since they thought
a garden is a grave, and drains the inkwell.
Theirs, Victorian England's one true marriage,
one Victorian England pronounced *Mormonage;*
a match between two writers. Writers marry
their kind still, true and one and clashing, though lacking
the woman's dull gray eyes, vast pendulous nose,
her huge mouth, and jawbone which forbore to finish:
George Eliot's gracious, indifferent Tolstoyan gaze,
George Eliot without Tolstoy, the Countess Tolstoy.

6. *The Book of Wisdom*

Can I go on loving anyone at fifty,
still cool to the brief and five-times wounded lives
of those we loathed with wild idealism young?
Though the gods only toss me twenty cards,
twenty, thirty, or fifty years of work,
I shiver up vertical like a baby pigeon,
palate-sprung for the worm, senility—
to strap the gross artillery to my back,
lash on destroying what I lurch against,
not with anger, but unwieldy feet,
ballooning like the spotted, warty, blow-rib toad,
King Solomon croaking, "This too is vanity;
her lips are a scarlet thread, her breasts are towers,"
hymns of the terrible organ in decay.

7. Descendant

The cloud of witnesses . . . they are flown like sundew,
and have left their debts to the widow and orphan;
to the virus crawling on its belly like a blot,
a hairbreadth an aeon, lives of love-in-death,
Venusberg in Venus fly-trap; to the tyrannosaur,
first carnivore to stand on its own feet,
to the Piltdown Man, first carnivore to laugh;
to the raised hand of Hitler, clenched fist of Stalin—
heaven descending from the hand of man.
But was there some shining, grasping hand to guide
me when I breathed through gills, and walked on fins
through Eden, plucking the law of retribution from the tree?
Did the Lord wish to enjoy the desolation,
the snake in the garden, an agent provocateur?

8. Bird

Aroused, then sleeping, caught adrift . . . the voice
singing to me in French, *"O mon avril."*
Those nasals . . . they woo us. Spring. Not theirs. Not mine.
A large pileated bird flies up,
dropping excretions like a frightened snake,
its Easter feathers; its earwax-yellow spoonbill
angrily hitting from side to side to blaze
a broad passage through the Great Northern Jungle—
the lizard tyrants were killed to a man by this bird,
man's forerunner. I pick up stones, and hope
to snatch its crest, its crown, at last, and cross
the perilous passage, sound in mind and body . . .
often reaching the passage, seeing my thoughts
stream on the water, as if I were cleaning fish.

(57)

Mexico

1

The difficulties, the impossibilities,
stand out: I, fifty, humbled with the years' gold garbage,
dead laurel grizzling my back like spines of hay;
you, some sweet, uncertain age, say twenty-seven,
unballasted by honor or deception.
What help then? Not the sun, the scarlet blossom,
and the high fever of this seventh day,
the wayfarer's predestined diarrhea, nausea,
the multiple mosquito spots, round as pesos.
Hope not in God here, nor the Aztec gods;
we sun-people know the sun, the source of life,
will die, unless we feed it human blood—
we two are clocks, and only count in time;
the hand's knife-edge is pressed against the future.

2

Faith that neither quickstep, nor slowstep, nor charges fanned
by the flame of Allah, nor hope of saving wife and child
weigh much against their concentrated fire—
Abel learned this falling among the jellied
green creepers and morning-glories of the saurian sunset.
Stand still, you'll feel the sureness, the delirium,
rank and file certain of smashing the enemy,
Dundee's clans at Killicrankie, who broke
the English, so three days later they were still running.
We're knotted together in innocence and guile;
yet we are not equal; I have lived without
sense so long the loss no longer hurts;
reflex and the ways of the world will float me free—
you, God help you, must will each breath you take.

(58)

3

Wishing to raise the cross of the Crucified King
in the monastery of Emmaus at Cuernavaca—
world names for their avant-garde crucifixes
and streamlined silver, the monks, like Paul, had earned
the cost of depth-transference by their craft.
A Papal Commission camped on them two years,
ruling analysis cannot be compulsory,
their cool Belgian prior was heretical, a fairy. . . .
We couldn't find the corpse removed by helicopter;
the cells were empty, but the art still sold;
lay-neurotics peeped out at you like deer,
barbwired in spotless whitewashed cabins, named
Sigmund and *Karl*. . . . They live the life of monks,
one revelation healing the ravage of the other.

4

The lizard rusty as a leaf rubbed rough
does nothing for days but puff his throat
for oxygen, and tongue up the passing flies,
sees only similar rusty lizards pant:
harems worthy this lord of the universe—
each thing he does generic, and not the best.
But how fragrantly our cold hands warm to the live coal!
We sit on the cliff like curs, chins pressed to thumbs,
the Toltec temples changing to dust in the dusk—
hair of the vulture, white brow of the moon: this too dust . . .
dust out of time, two clocks set back to the Toltec Eden,
as if we still wished to pull teeth with firetongs—
when they took a city, they too murdered everything:
man, woman and child, down to the pigs and dogs.

5

South of New England, south of Washington,
south of the South, I walk the glazed moonlight:
dew on the grass and nobody about . . .
drawn on by my unlimited desire,
like a bull with a ring in its nose and a chain in the ring. . . .
We moved far, bull and cow, could one imagine
cattle obliviously pairing for six long days:
up road and down, then up again this same
bricked garden road, stiff spines of hay stuck in our hides;
and always in full sight of everyone,
of the full sun, of the silhouetting sunset,
shown up by the undimmed lights of the passing car.
Then gone; I am learning to live in history.
What is history? What you cannot touch.

6

Midwinter in Mexico, yet the tall red flowers
stand up on many trees, and all's in leaf;
twilight bakes the wall-brick large as a loaf of bread—
somewhere I must have met this feverish pink before,
and knew its message; or is it that I walk
you home twenty times, and then turn back on my tracks?
No moment comes back to hand, not twice, not once.
We've waited, I think, a lifetime for this walk,
and the white powder beneath our feet slides out
like the sterile white salt of purity; even
your puffed lace blouse is salt. The bricks glide; the commonest
minute is not divided, not twice, not once. . . .
When you left, I thought of you each hour of the day,
each minute of the hour, each second of the minute.

(60)

7

Three pillows, end on end, and rolled in the daybed
blanket—elastic, curved and cool. For a second,
by some hallucination of the hand,
I thought I was unwrapping you. In the twilight,
the lavatory breathes out its sweet and shocking perfume,
Coca-Cola laced with rum. Dark, dear, dark:
here always, the night's illusory, houselights
watch Mexicans, mostly kids, squared up by boxlike
houses on a street where buses eat up the sidewalk.
And New Year's midnight: three in the market drink beer
from cans garnished with limes and salt; one woman, Aztec,
sings her adultery ballads, and weeps because
her husband has left her for three women—to face
the poverty all men must face at the hour of death.

8

As if we chewed dry twigs and salt grasses,
filling our mouths with dust and bits of adobe,
lizards, rats and worms, we walk downhill,
love demanding we be calm, not lawful,
for laws imprison as much as they protect.
Six stone lions, hard drinkers, more like frogs,
guarding the fountain; three rusted arc-lights, rusting;
four stone inkfish, thrice stepped on, lifting the spout—
not starred in any guidebook . . . this city of the plain,
where the water turns red, as if it were dyed,
and thirteen girls sit at the barroom table,
then none, then only twenty coupled men,
homicidal with morality and lust—
devotion hikes uphill in iron shoes.

(61)

9

Looking about me with the strength of three,
three men, two women, or one unmarried, I see
the two immovable nuns, out of habit, too fat to leave
the dormitory, living for ten days on tea,
bouillon cubes, cookies bought and brought from Boston.
You curl in your metal bunk-bed like my child,
I sprawl at your elbow pillowed from the dead floor—
nuns packing, nuns ringing the circular iron stair,
nuns in pajamas scalloped through their wrappers,
nuns boiling bouillon, tea or cookies—nuns
brewing and blanketing reproval. . . .
The soul groans and laughs at its lack of stature—
if you want to make the frozen serpent dance,
you must sing it the music of its mouth.

10

No artist perhaps, you go beyond their phrases,
a girl too simple for this measured cunning. . . .
Take that day of baking on the marble veranda,
the roasting brown rock, the roasting brown grass, the breath
of the world risen like the ripe smoke of chestnuts,
a cleavage dropping miles to the valley's body;
and the following sick and thoughtful day
of the red flower, the hills, the valley, the Volcano—
this not the greatest thing, though great; the hours
of shivering, ache and burning, when we'd charged
so far beyond our courage—altitudes,
then the falling . . . falling back on honest speech:
infirmity, a food the flesh must swallow,
feeding our minds . . . the mind which is also flesh.

11

Sounds of a popping bonfire; no, a colleague's
early typing; or is he needing paregoric?
Poor Child, you were kissed so much you thought you were walked
yet you wait in my doorway with bluebells in your hair.　　　[on;
Those other *yous,* you think, are they meaningless *in toto,*
test-rockfalls you crudely approached and coarsely conquered,
leaving no juice in the flaw, mind lodged in mind?
Those others, those *yous* . . . a child wants everything—
things! A child, though earnest, is not quite mortal.
Love blots the categories; yet men trust
love's way is always through the common garden. . . .
I ask only coolness, stillness, intercourse—
sleep wastes the day lifelong behind your eyes,
night shivers at noonday in the boughs of the fir.

12

To clasp, not grasp the life and light and fragile;
as the intermeshing limbs of Lucifer
sink to sleep on the tumuli of Lilith. . . .
We're burnt, black chips knocked from the blackest stock:
Potato-famine Irish-Puritan, and Puritan—
gold made them smile like pigs once, then fear of falling—
hipbones finer than a breast of a squab,
eyes hard as stars, hearts small as elves, they turned
the wilderness to wood, then looked for trees.
They are still looking. Now our hesitant
conversation moves from lust to love;
friendship, without dissension, multiplying
days, days, days, days—how can I love you more,
short of turning into a criminal?

Canterbury

Regret those jousting aristocracies,
war-bright, though useless, their lives a round of games;
sex horsed their chivalry, even when
the aggressor was only an artless dragon. . . .
The Black Prince folds a missal in his hands,
rests, stone-chainmail, *imprimatur,* on his slab.
Suppression hardened to his gallantry;
behind the spasms of his ruffian hand,
slept a public school and sober faith in murder.
Here the worn pilgrim and kneeling savant ask:
"Do I have the right to imagination?"
Here the great fighter Captain lies with those
who made it, those whom fate disdained to wound.
All's dull here, all's peace here; theirs the new day.

Killicrankie

The Scotch Lords once had means to salmon fish,
the painter means to paint them playing salmon,
gray crag, sunrise or sunset, brawling tarn,
poachers stripped, gashed, parceled to the birds—
if we do not fight, we had better break up and die.
In the Highlands, wherever war is not a science,
we humbly ask for nerve in our commander.
Ours kicked off the one pair of shoes in the clan
to walk us barefoot. The British drank the grass;
torrents of their redcoats and tartans raving down
the valley to the gorge of Killicrankie.
Dundee's cuirass rose; still, he waved his sword,
he'd won the battle, lost his life and Scotland.
"If it's well with the King, it matters little to me."

Midwinter

1. Friend across Central Park

Home from you, and through the trodden tangle,
the corny birdwalk, the pubescent knoll,
the dirtwood rowboats docked three deep, the tundra
between past Eightieth Street to under Seventieth,
snow mucking to pepper and salt, to brain-cell dull,
to ink . . . to winter throwing off its decorations
on Manhattan, and on this day, in twenty minutes
inked from light to night—I thinking without pause
of you in Eisenhower's Washington,
I in my Dickensian muffler, snow-sugared, unraveling—
so you phantasized—in the waste thaw of loss:
winter and then a winter; unseared, your true voice seared,
still yearningly young; and I, though never young
in all our years, am younger when we meet.

2. Another Friend

Nothing less necessary than a girl shining a mirror,
waiting the miracle of the polishing winds,
mirrors turning dark to the leaf of May. . . .
You were not very wise, or unique in any skill;
not unreasonably, heaven became your enemy,
you knew your shadow to be the coming night;
knew from the steam of dried straw, the barn would burn.
I didn't want you to be warmed by walking,
each drop of perspiration on your face,
an admiring eye. . . . Why do I remember
your galled young fingers and blood-drenched ink,
that scar of an unfulfilled desire to be,
the happiness of the drop to die in the river? . . .
The wave of the wineglass trembled to see you walk.

(66)

3. *Judith*

"The Latins are much like Arabs, as we say at Radcliffe;
decay of infeud scattered the Scottish clans,
but ours is an airier aristocracy:
professors, statesmen, new art, old, the city
where only Jews can write an English sentence,
the Jewish mother, half wasp, half anti-wasp,
says, *liberate, literate, liberalize!*
If her boy dies and takes his lay in state,
she calms the grandeur of his marble hair.
Like Judith, she would cut the Virgin Mary
or Marie-Antoinette or Mary Stuart
leftist-Tsarists, jet-set parachutes;
knowing a lightweight is like knowing Holofernes—
smack! her sword divorced the codshead from the codspiece."

4. *The Goldfish*

The biggest cat sees all through eyefilm, yawns
dreamily, "Such a sweet young radical couple!"
She prays for the man to come without his wife.
The decks of windows graze on Central Park,
from such elevation the crowd is part of a movie,
and money flies in airmail to meet the rent.
"Is it as Marx dreamed, man is what he makes?"
she sighs. "The rich have muscle." The windows face
the unilluminating city lights,
as a goldfish might estimate the universe.
She sees the old left yielding place to new,
and eyes her guest, young, dissident, a trustee;
and tonight he is single, he has everything,
swims in her like an eel in the Bay of Fundy.

(67)

5. *Elisabeth Schwarzkopf in New York*

Yet people live here . . . Paris, Wien, Milano,
which had more genius, grace, preoccupations?
We pass up grace, our entrance fee and tithe
for dwelling in the heavenly Jerusalem—
small price for salience, and the world is here:
Elisabeth Schwarzkopf sings, herself her parts,
Wo ist Silvia and *die Marschallin,*
until the rivers of the early world,
the Hudson and the Tigris, burst their bar,
trembling like water-ivy down the spine,
from the satyr's tussock to his hardened hoof—
la Diva, crisped, remodeled for the boards,
roughs it with chaff and cardigan at recordings,
is anyone's single and useful weekend guest.

6. *Across the Yard: La Ignota*

The soprano's bosoms point to the joy of God,
Brunhild who would not rule her voice for God—
she has to sing to fill such windows, hang
such drapes: one is pink dust flipped back to scarlet,
the other besmirched gauze—behind the first,
a blown electric heater; behind the second,
and placed as furniture, her footlocker
with Munich stickers. No one really hires her;
her grandiose, arched wooden window frames
haven't felt paint or putty these twenty years;
grass, dead since Kennedy, chokes the window box.
Like a grackle, she flings her high aria through the trash. . . .
When I was lost and green, I would have given
the janitor three months' rent for this address.

School

1. For Peter Taylor

That doleful Kenyon snapshot: you ham-squat on your bed,
jaw hung sidewise, and your eyes too glossy;
chest syrup, wicked greens of diesel oil;
you the same sickly green, except you are
transparent. I can almost touch and smell
those pajamas we were too brush-off to change,
and wore as winter underwear through our trousers.
When the snapshot was developed, I saw you couldn't
live a week, and thought you might have died,
squatting upright, a last dynasty mummy.
You live on: earth's obliquities of health,
though Adams knew the Southerner must go under—
love teases. We're one still, we are weaker, wilder—
stuck in one room again, we want to fight.

2. Randall Jarrell

The dream went like a rake of sliced bamboo,
slats of the dust distracted by downdraw;
I woke and knew I held a cigarette;
I looked, there was none, could have been none;
I slept the years now, and I woke again,
palming the floor, shaking the sheets. I found
nothing smoking. I am awake, I see
the cigarette burn safely in my fingers . . .
They come this path, old friends, old buffs of death.
Tonight it's Randall, the spark of fire though humbled,
his gnawed wrist cradled like his *Kitten*. "What kept you so long,
racing your cooling grindstone to ambition?
Surely this life was fast enough . . . But tell me,
Cal, why did we live? Why do we die?"

Lines from Israel

1. World War I, 1916

"I am beginning to rub my eyes at the prospect of peace,
when we will have to know the dead are not
dead only for the duration of the war;
I am in glowing looks, I've never seen
myself in such keen color, and most by daylight . . .
Strange to know suddenly in this slowly farewell war
that I know many more dead than I know living . . ."
Turning the page in *Time* to see her picture,
expecting some London Judith, *no trespass,*
I touch your green shutter-sweater and breathing breasts:
Lady Cynthia Asquith, the undying bulwark of British girl . . .
The word miracle was less common there than here,
yet sleeping with this one might not have been maneuvered—
each stone an acre, or unexploded minefield.

March, 1969

2. Sands of the Desert

The vagabond Alexander passed here, *romero—*
here in Israel, or here in the Near East? Near what?
A dry wind bleeds the driven telephone lines;
the province, still provincial, prays to the One God
who left his footmark on a field of blood . . .
And wherever the sun fermented man from dust
our blood leaps up in friendship like a cold spring . . .
Alexander learned to share the earth with God,
and God to live for heaven—a shrivelled distance,
his face an azure sand-dollar on the pail of a child . . .
And each season some active ruler, some Ahab, says,
"If my enemies would only see me, I am safe."
But the good murderer is always blind;
the leopard entered the Ark and keeps his spots.

Writers

1. T. S. Eliot

Caught between two streams of traffic, in the gloom
of Memorial Hall and Harvard's war-dead. . . . And he:
"Don't you loathe to be compared with your relatives?
I do. I've just found two of mine reviewed by Poe.
He wiped the floor with them . . . and I was *delighted*."
Then on with warden's pace across the Yard,
talking of Pound, "It's balls to say he isn't
the way he is. . . . He's better though. This year,
he no longer wants to rebuild the Temple at Jerusalem.
Yes, he's better. '*You* speak,' he said, when he'd talked two hours.
By then I had absolutely nothing to *say*."
Ah Tom, one muse, one music, had one the luck—
lost in the dark night of the brilliant talkers,
humor and boredom from the everlasting dross!

2. Ezra Pound

Horizontal in a deckchair on the bleak ward,
some feeble-minded felon in pajamas, clawing
a Social Credit broadside from your table, you saying,
". . . here with a black suit and black briefcase; in the briefcase,
an abomination, Possum's *hommage* to Milton."
Then sprung; Rapallo, and then the decade gone;
then three years, then Eliot dead, you saying,
"And who is left to understand my jokes?
My old Brother in the arts . . . and besides, he was a smash of a
He showed us his blotched, bent hands, saying, "Worms.   [poet."
When I talked that nonsense about Jews on the Rome
wireless, she knew it was shit, and still loved me."
And I, "Who else has been in Purgatory?"
And he, "To begin with a swelled head and end with swelled feet."

3. *Ford Madox Ford*

Taking in longhand Ford's dictation on Provence,
the great Prosateur swallowing his Yorkshire British,
I fishing for what he said each second sentence—
"You have no ear," he'd say, "for the Lord's prose,
Shakespeare's medium: *No king, be his cause never so spotless,
will try it out with all unspotted soldiers.*"
I brought him my loaded and overloaded lines.
He said, "You have your butterfly existence:
half hour of work, two minutes to love, the rest boredom.
Conrad spent a day finding the *mot juste;* then killed it."
In time, he thought, I might live to be an artist.
"Most of them are born to fill the graveyards."
"If he fails as a writer," Ford wrote my father, "at least
he'll be Ambassador to England, or President of Harvard."

4. *To Allen Tate I*

My longest drive, two hundred miles, it seemed:
Nashville to Clarksville to the River Cumberland,
March 1937, in *my* month Pisces,
Europe's last fling of impotence and anger—
and above your fire the blood-crossed flag of the States,
a Stonewall Jackson, a twenty-two at half-cock—
you routing the windmills with only a gamecock's warcries.
And the moonshine was as white as water;
tall, dirty, stately setpieces in Southern patois;
saying your tenant with ten children had more art
than Thomas Wolfe. And, "Do they expect me to leave the South
to meet frivolous people like Tugwell and Mrs. Roosevelt?"
Ford, playing Russian Banker in that half-light, sneering,
"You must show your cards, dear Tate . . . it isn't done."

(72)

5. *To Allen Tate II*

On your enormous brow, cannonball head of a snowman,
is a ripped red tissuepaper birthday hat;
you squint, make out my daughter, then six or seven:
"*You* are a Southern *belle;* do you know why
you are a *South*ern belle?" (Stares, stupor, thumb in her mouth)
"Because your *mother* is a Southern belle."
Your attention wanders, "I love you now, but I'll love you
more probably when you are older." Harriet whispering,
"If you are still alive." We reach Gettysburg;
both of us too much the soldier from Sourmash:
"I don't know whether to call you my son or my brother."
Ashtrays and icecubes deployed as Pickett's columns:
a sloping forest of flashing steel. You point:
"There, if Longstreet had *moved,* we would have *broke* you."

6. *William Carlos Williams*

Whom would I love more? William Carlos Williams,
in collegiate black slacks, gabardine coat,
and loafers polished like the rosewood on yachts,
straying stonefoot through his town-end garden,
man and flower seedy with three autumn strokes,
his brown, horned eyes enlarged, an ant's, through glasses;
the Mother, stonedeaf, her face a wrinkled talon,
burnt-out ash of her long-haired Puerto Rican grasses;
the black, blind, bituminous eye is inquisitorial.
"Mama," he says, "which would you rather see here,
us or three blondes?" Then later, "The old bitches
live into their hundreds, while I'll kick off tomorrow."
And saying, "I am sixty-seven, and more
attractive to girls than when I was seventeen."

7. Robert Frost

Robert Frost at midnight, the audience gone
to vapor, the great act laid on the shelf in mothballs,
his voice musical, raw and raw—he writes in the flyleaf:
"Robert Lowell from Robert Frost, his friend in the art."
"Sometimes I feel too full of myself," I say.
And he, misunderstanding, "When I am low,
I stray away. My son wasn't your kind. The night
we told him Merrill Moore would come to treat him,
he said, 'I'll kill him first.' One of my daughters thought things,
knew every male she met was out to make her;
the way she dresses, she couldn't make a whorehouse."
And I, "Sometimes I'm so happy I can't stand myself."
And he, "When I am too full of joy, I think
how little good my health did anyone near me."

Those Older

1

They won't stay gone, rising with royal torpor,
as if held in my binoculars' fog and enlargement,
casting the raindrops of the rainbow: children;
loved by their still older elders in a springtide
invisible to us as the Hittites. We're too near now
to date their comings and goings—those *late* people:
Cousin Susie and Cousin Belle. Fate stamped
them with their maiden name *for life*—blood-rich,
and constellations from the dancing heart.
Our first to die . . . so odd and light and dry,
they seemed foreshadows of some earlier, strange creation,
hooded in snail-shells, the unassailable
deafness of their formidable asperity—
our girls . . . less than a toy, and more than a flower.

2

Another was a man in his middle life
from the days of his youth till the day of his death;
and yet the matching of his fresh-cut flowers
was over-delicate and dead for death,
as if the flowery coverlet lay like lead,
asserting that no primitive ferment
or slobbering poignance of the voyeur God
would ever corrupt or soil his earthly vestment
spread like King Solomon in the Episcopal morgue,
sanguine, still ready for his thousand lovers. . . .
Here at world's end, here with nowhere else to go,
lie those before us, and those just before us:
less than a toy, and more than a flower . . .
rich and poor, the poor . . . no trees in the sky.

3

No fence stands up between us and our object:
approaching nearer, nailing down the old,
and free to pick those neither ripe nor young,
as the hollow green wilderness sings the guillotine,
sings those before us. . . . I have had them fifty years:
all those grander, or finer, or simply older,
gone astraying down a backward street, the trees,
late-lopped, tar-boned, old prunes like stumps of martyrs;
and even this dead timber is bulldozed rootless,
and we face faceless lines of white frame houses,
sanded, stranded, undarkened by shade or shutter—
rich and poor . . . no trees in the sky—their stones,
so close they melt to a field of snow, as we pass,
won from the least desire to have what is.

Ice on the Hudson

1

The air is snow-touched, fans our streaming backs,
blows in and in, a thousand snow-years back;
we were joined in love a thousand snow-years back.
Snow purifies the air that breathes our flesh,
waterfall white of China flays the glass;
but this is dream, no storm dare set a foot in,
blown spray nor wave can reach our stilted window.
Will the white foam-wisp soil with poison when it hits
the Hudson's prone and essence-steaming back,
the Great Arriviste in the metropolis?
Manhattan is pierced by the stiletto heel—
this too a dream; New York was never a person. . . .
In the days of the freeze, we see a minor sun,
our winter moon bled for the solar rose.

2

They too have had their saints and Roundhead cells
to guide them down the narrow path and true,
home to desolation and regimental terror—
a gunman father . . . theirs was something of an artist
at his vague, dreamlike trade of blood and guile—
one joke meant death—meat stuck between that tooth
and gum began to stink in half a second. . . .
Ah the rain rains down in drops like iron balls;
the River's ice-jammed; miserable Manhattan
stands on stilts to the taunts of its ice-black heaven.
O when will we sleep out the storm, dear love,
say to the minute, stop for good, stop dead,
see at the end of our walk some girl's burnt-yellow legs
glow, as if she had absorbed the sun?

My Death

1

Reading this book to four or five that night
at Cuernavaca, till the lines glowered and glowed,
and my friend, Monsignor Illich, ascetic donkey,
braying, "Will you die, when the book is done?"
It stopped my heart, and not my mouth. I said,
"I have begun to wonder." Old lapsed R.C.,
lacking half-way to atheist, I knew
I must pay for these opportunist violations.
Or was his *die: as if,* his gracenote saying,
"It is writing, if you run, as if to die."
Christ's first portrait is a donkey's head,
the simple truth is in his simple word,
lies buried in a random, haggard sentence,
cutting ten ways to nothing clearly carried.

2

The dream of changing costume, set and cast,
all working more for character than life—
it is a sort of Cambridge for the arts,
though none I meet are artists, only people.
At the end of the round of visits, at rope's-end,
I soak at the high table without tablecloth,
talking to someone presently my father.
His hair, grown richer, peacocks out in bangs;
"I do it," he says, "to look manlier and younger.
I have had to sink all my spare money in courses:
music and singing, and my trusty math."
Had to? We are joined in the arts, though old;
"I have never loved you so much in all our lives."
And he, "Doesn't it begin at the beginning?"

February and March

1. Cows

The cows of Potter and Albert Cuyp are timeless;
in the depths of Europe, we find their scrawly pastures
and scrawlier hamlets unwatered by paint or Hegel,
the benighted provincial kirk. None of our rear-guard painters,
the lover of nature, the hater of abstraction,
can do these landscapes. With a bull's watery eye,
dewlap and misty phallus, Cuyp caught the farthest glisten,
tonnage and rumination of the sod.
And there is a whiteness; behind your sixties dress,
feudal vassal's workday, and R.C. morals,
lies the windfall abandon of Giorgione,
Renaissance idleness—only the lovely,
the good, the wealthy served the Venetian, whose art
knew nothing yet of husbandry and cattle.

2. The Golden Middle

The ceiling is twenty feet above our heads;
oak panels, mantel and oak linoleum tiles;
book-ladders on brass rods and rollers touch the sky—
in middle age, the good costs less and less. . . .
Who can deduct these years? Become a student,
graced with rebellion, hair and the caw of Shelley,
his hectic hopes, his tremulous success,
the ignominious and bitter death?
Here the hard, cunning light would leave his eyes,
soon he would starve his genius for denial,
hear a song in the pipes, the chirp of frogs,
and turn with the tread of an ox to serve the rich,
clinging to status, police and private schools
to lift their feet from the mud of the republic.

3. *Vigil*

Famine's joy is in the enjoyment; who'll deny
the crash, delirious uterus living it up?
Therefore, we lie here, in heat or cold—heat knocking,
winter brushing the window white with frost.
It's not good moments, but the town defruited
gives us the toothache . . . to destroy a people
for its own good, and let the world go by:
green year, a green year, twenty percent for peace,
now down to ten or nine. We breathe, we live,
since our death is useless to killed or killing,
since the window shatters and the wind is blowing,
since the trees are leafless and the boughs are green,
the hunters hunted. . . . Why do we live and breathe—
tough as the cat, nine lives to go, then none?

4. *Le Cygne*

The virgin, the blind, the beautiful today,
dares it break the mirror of this lake,
hard, neglectful, hoarding under ice
a great glacier of flights that never fly?
The swan worsens, remembers it is he,
the magnificence that gives itself no hope,
the fortitude that finds no *raison d'être*—
the great boredoms blaze in the sterile winter.
The whole neck shakes in this white agony
inflicted by the space the swan denies;
he cannot deny the ice that ties his feet.
His pure brilliance led him to this grand asylum,
governed by staccato cries of grandeur,
pride that clothes the swan in useless exile.

5. Thirst

We have taken too much salt here—thirst without
bottom; young we dug acid from the saltmarsh;
your hand, a small monkey's, cannot scratch our names;
the chilling glass of julep blows to pollen.
There'll be no more. Some can escape in sleep;
they find their tunnel, and its only exit,
a hole soon filled with twenty slides of rock;
the oxygen expires; we hope the wind will rush
through a smashed window, that Faith will move the mountain.
Who has met death with warmth? I know, it's like that:
in love, forgetting. Few are able to love,
bear their bearers, the never to be forgotten
my father, *my* mother . . . these names, this function, given
by them once, given existence now by us.

6. Helltime

Our God; he walks with us, he talks with us,
in sleep, in thunder, and in wind and weather;
he strips the wind and gravel from our words,
and speeds us naked on the single way.
Is he the winds, or is it revelation,
the time-bomb buried in this ton of trash?
The servants are degraded by rebuff,
desertions such as they too dealt in solitary.
In some Bolivian tin mine we, the servants,
drop-outs, hoop-spines, lock hands and haul together;
God finds no profit in descending here,
finds only smear, expendables of love,
nothing and helltime borne by faithful servants,
the flatterer's all-forgiving, wounded smile.

7. Utopia for Racoons

My goiter expert smiles like a racoon,
"O.K., you're rich and can afford to die."
Claws me a minute, claws his notes for five,
claws me a day, then claws the notes for five;
could crack an adam's-apple like a walnut.
The doctor washes, licks his paws of me,
and sips his fountainpen for bubbly ink.
On a second floor in a second hospital,
two racoons wear stethoscopes to count the pulse
of their geiger-counter and their thyroid scan;
they sit sipping my radioactive iodine
from a small lead bottle with two metal straws,
"What little health we have is stolen fruit.
What is the life-expectancy of a racoon?"

8. Fame

We bleed for people, so independent and selfsuspicious,
if the door is locked, they just come back, instead of knocking—
hearts scarred by complaints they would not advance;
it was not their good fortune to meet their love;
however long they lived, they would still be waiting.
We believed you, they said, by believing you were lying. . . .
Timur saying something like: "The drop of water
that fails to become a river is food for the dust";
or "The eye that cannot size up the whole of the Tigris
in a drop is a child's game, not the eye of a man. . . ."
His face in the mirror was like the sun on a dewdrop;
the path of death is always underfoot;
this the sum of the world's scattered elements—
fame, a bouquet in the niche of forgetfulness!

(82)

9. *Growing in Favor*

This waking with a start of pathos to fear—
it comes too often now, though no less often
in the year of my first razor and the death of God;
thick then my tongue, as if anesthetized,
a fish, silk-screened, gaped air into a bubble,
red rose, wallpaper rose, drank dank plaster, turned a cabbage,
my blood clung to me, stuck, a thorn in blossom. . . .
A little further on, and I am nature:
my pinch of dust lies on the eternal dust-tray,
lies on call forever, never called. . . .
Who will call for me, call girl, when I start awake,
all my diminishment retarded, wake
to sing the dawnless alba of the gerontoi? . . .
Old age is all right, but it has no future.

10. *Last Summer*

Asleep just now, just now I am awake,
see a man designed on the back of a card:
his trousers, laundered green; his coat, wet leaf;
his fair young flesh, sky-green of the deep vein.
I turn the card, the figure clears to trees and grass—
last summer for the wondered mind . . . for seeing
the dead servant's green turf beyond the pale,
white marble mantel, bust, rolled rug, the sheeted den,
the old master covered with his pillowslip—
searching as everyman for my one good deed,
crying love lost in the long apprenticeship:
friend, wife or child, their vanished art of breathing;
knowing I must forget how to breathe through my mouth,
now I am dead, and just now I was made.

(83)

11. *Cranach's Man-Hunt*

Composed, you will say, for our ever friendship,
almost one arm around our many shoulders,
one shade darkens the stream of the photograph,
friends bound by birth and accent . . . we had one.
We're game for the deer-hunt, ages five to ninety,
seniority no cipher to who will die
on this clearing of blown, tame grass, a trap of landscape,
green bow in the bend of the choppy, lavender stream,
eighteen or nineteen of us, bounding or swimming,
hurt stags and does . . . the Kaiser Maximilian
and the wise Saxon Elector, screened by one clump,
winching their crossbows . . . the horsemen, picadors,
whipped to action by their beautiful, verminous dogs,
to this battle the Prince has never renounced or lost.

12. *First Spring*

After a year, I almost breathe-in rain,
horseclopping down fire-escape to skylight to black
court-cobble downward; the rain renews. Not here,
till spring, the snakehead, breaks the yielding cake;
a reek, not smell, of life. For whom? For what?
For the horses, six bets in ten misplaced,
when other younger generations face
the firing squads, and our blood is wiped from the pavement.
For our passive courage, paralysis
that held us upright like tenpins to face the strike—
Coleridge's laudanum and brandy,
his alderman's stroll to positive negation—
his large plant with pith within, not heart of wood,
power without strength, an involuntary impostor.

(84)

13. *Rembrandt*

His faces crack . . . if mine could crack and breathe!
His Jewish Bridegroom, palm spread on the Jewish Bride's
bashful, taffeta-leveled bosom, is faithful;
   the fair girl, slum background, gives soul to his flayed steer.
Her breasts, the snowdrop, won't hold water;
   those Dutch were sad sacks, all their women bags,
   obstinate, undefeated hull of the old scow.
But Bathsheba's ample stomach, her heavy, practical feet,
are reverently dried by the faithful servant,
his eyes dwell lovingly on each baggy pucker,
her unfortunate body is the privilege of his service,
the radiance of his spirit void of possession. . . .
One sees, if one sees at all, through a red mist
the strange new idol of the marketplace.

Pastime

1

Unorthodox sleep in the active hour:
young afternoon; the room, half-darkened, is day;
a raw draft is brushing sock and sole.
Like cells of a charging battery, I charge up sleep—
if such sleep lasts, I touch eternity.
This, its pulse-stop, must have been before.
What is true is not real: I here, this bed here, this hour here,
this day, not bright or blinds; impenetrable
brute truth free with reason like our flesh.
Voices drop from forms of distant apartments,
voices of schoolboys . . . they are always ours,
early prep-school; just as this hour is always
optional recess—this has been before:
the sting of touching past time by dropping off.

2

Labor to pull the raw breath through my closed nostrils
brings back breathing another, rawer air,
drawn freely enough from frozen-crust football,
sunlight gilding the golden polo coats
of boys with country seats on the Dutch Hudson.
But why does that light stay? First Form football,
first time being sent on errands by a schoolmate—
Bobby Delano, cousin of Franklin Delano Roosevelt,
escorted drunk off the Presidential yacht,
winner of the football and hockey letters at fifteen;
at fifteen, expelled. He dug my ass with a compass,
and forced me to say my mother was a whore.
My freshman year, he shot himself in Rio,
odious, unknowable, inspired as Ajax.

(86)

April 8, 1968

1. Two Walls

Somewhere a white wall faces a white wall,
one wakes the other, the other wakes the first,
each burning in the other's borrowed splendor—
the walls, once woken, are forced to go on talking,
their color looks much alike, two shadings of white,
each living in the shadow of the other.
How fine these distinctions when we cannot choose!
Don Giovanni must have drawn sword on such an avenger,
two contracting, white stone walls—their pursuit
of happiness and his, coincident. . . .
At this point of civilization, this point of the world,
the only satisfactory companion we
can imagine is death—this morning, skin lumping in my throat,
I lie here, heavily breathing, the soul of New York.

2. Words of a Young Girl

"Trees broomed before our rosewood bungalow,
not real ones, these were tropical, and straw;
the Gulf fell like a shower on the fiber-sand;
it wasn't ocean like our northern coast,
unfit for swimming. We met a couple, not people,
shades asking Father whether he was his name—
none ever said that I was Harriet.
They were laying a beach-fire, and the sticks were guns;
our little bungalow was burning—it
had burned, and we were in it, yet the barrels
were only firecrackers made of scarlet cardboard;
the shots were froth, the fire was fizz. . . . Months later,
we scrubbed away our scars and blisters, unable
to answer if we had ever hurt."

(87)

3. *The Petit Bourgeois*

Our floor, ganged, liberated, not yet fire—
hand over hand on the one knotted rope, the boy,
a cool crew haircut, tans above the ledge,
smiling at me to mount his shoulders, swing
down fifty tiers of windows, two city blocks,
on that frail thread, that singed and swinging rope,
our building from here, a tapered, swaying rope,
fat in the head and narrow at the base,
face mirrored pear-shaped in a silver spoon.
You must go down the rope to save your life;
long ago, this was answered by hallucination:
if forced to walk to safety on a tightrope,
if my life swung on my will and skill . . . better to die.
The crowds in the street were cheering, when we refused.

Mania

1. *1958*

Remember standing with me in the dark,
Ann Adden? In the wild house? Everything—
I mad, you mad for me? And brought my ring,
that twelve-carat lunk of gold there . . . my Joan of Arc,
undeviating then from the true mark—
robust, ah taciturn! Remember our playing
Marian Anderson in Mozart's *Shepherd King,*
Il Re Pastore there? O Hammerheaded Shark,
the Rainbow Salmon of the World, your hand
a rose—not there, a week earlier! We stand. . . .
We ski-walked the eggshell at the Mittersill,
Pascal's infinite, perfect, fearful sphere—
the border nowhere, your center everywhere. . . .
And if I forget you, Ann, may my right hand . . .

2. *1968*

"Dear Lowell, sitting sixty feet above the sea,
hearing my father build a house on this cliff,
sixty feet above the Penobscot Bay,
returning here from my ten years in Europe,
waiting for emigration papers, work cards etc.;
I chanced to read your book, *Near the Ocean.*
I'm older . . . an extending potency. . . .
What I'd like to say is humanity,
like the breezy Pharaohs the first Egyptians sculpted.
What I write to tell you is what a shining
remembrance of someone, of you, to hold of . . . me—
I aggrandize. . . . *1958;* now thundered
all the way through to that seemingly virginal time,
I fled America. We have a Viking son of three."

(89)

April

1. Roulette

Didn't Plato ban philosopher-professors,
the idols of the young, from the Republic?
And occupational republicans? It wasn't just
the artist. The Republic! But it never was,
except in the sky-ether of Plato's thought,
steam from the ordure of his city-state.
His roulette wheel repeats; the man in the street
is mobile—never since Adam delved, such plans,
Utopia on the roads to demolition.
This much still certain: whoever takes the sword
must die by the sword, or someone else will die;
it doesn't matter—injustice slays disorder—
it doesn't matter, new establishments
will serve the people, the people people serve.

2. Europa

The headache, the night of no performance, dusk of daybreak:
limping home by the fountain's Dionysiac gushes,
water smote from marble, the felon water,
the watery alcoholic going underground . . .
to the stone museum. But we were an empire, soul-brothers
to Babylon and China, their imperishable
hope to go beyond the growth of hope.
In the dark night of lust's defensive war,
your breasts were breathing—like your will to breathe;
we should have bred *in aeternum,* instead of doing nothing.
How many of your lovers never died?
While your breasts, white bull's-eyes cupped by your tan,
flatten on the leather and horn of Jupiter,
daring to raise his privates to the Godhead.

3. *Redskin*

Unsheathed, you unexpectedly go redskin,
except for two white torches, fruits of summer,
woman's headlights to guide us to the dark,
love of the body, the only love man knows.
Woman looks natural in herself, not man,
equipped with his redemptive bat and balls;
Renoir, paralyzed, painted with his penis,
did naked women, not Michelangelos.
Rain claws the door, a thousand fingernails;
your icy, poorly circulating fingers
trickle all night from heaven to the skin;
they will be warm by day, and we be warm—
at wrath-break, when the earth and ocean merge,
who wants to hold his weapon to the whale?

4. *Dalliance*

All was respectability, dark and secret,
dalliance means to dwell the hours of Eros—
this flower I take away and wear with fear;
who ever noticed? Othello never caught
Cassio reeking Desdemona's musk.
You grow more comforting, as you excite;
like the Macbeth murk of Manhattan in sunset smog.
Is it a hobby like heroin or birds?
Set at the helm, facing a pot of coals,
the sleet and wind spinning me ninety degrees,
I must not give me up then to the fire,
lest it invert my fire; it blinded me;
so did it me; there's wisdom that is woe,
but there is a woe that is madness.

5. *The Dialogue*

"One's family meetings in what new foreign bar?
Which lover is one's mother with this week?
Peers, womanizers, lifeguards, her great men,
almost by definition, were the jocks;
bantering insolence puffed the ponderous pigskin—
charging, they did not cheer or shout; they growled. . . ."
"But when I sought fame in my youth, I little knew
how near the catch was: books and vanity,
vast womb of echoes bound by injured nerve. . . .
Then I kept my ambition leashed, and only read it
to one or two friends." "You found a million friends.
In this short, indefinite time, I'll marry the least man,
the top of whose husbandry is raising flowers—
no sense in shouting the truth from the wrong window."

6. *The Misanthrope and the Painter*

"The misanthrope: a woman who hates man.
Women are stronger, but man is smarter." "Mostly
woman hates his drinking and his women,
hates this in all men; she will not permit
Cassio to escape tragedy."
"Hear the artist on her fellow artist,
woman on woman? 'The only way she can
repaint this one is for her to lie under a truck.'
I pick up lines from nothing." "I'm not nothing, Baby.
When I am in a room, Wyeth is invisible."
"When Rembrandt had painted the last spot of red
on his clown's nose, he disappeared in paint.
I pick lines from trash." "I'm not garbage, Baby.
You may have *joie de vivre,* but you're not twenty."

7. *Even Such*

"One step, two steps, one step, two steps, one step—
time takes our youth, our joys and all we have;
its First Commandment is to keep the step,
its Second is keep it up." "A noble nature
has no pocketwatch but the almanac;
let us throw out the clocks and live by the sun.
Christ might have lived forever, if he'd lived
from sun to sun, and slept the twelve-hour night."
"Our doctors know healthy sleeping leads to dying."
"But did anyone ever sleep with anyone
without thinking a split second he was God?"
"Even if such a one indiscreetly writes
the perfect sentence, he knows it isn't English.
Such a man wakes and sees his hair on the pillow."

8. *The White Goddess*

"I'm scratchy, I don't wear these epaulets
tacked to my chest for men to lift and haul.
As girls, we used to moon on the Amazon;
after the ten-hour treks, we snorted ten hours
or more, we had to let our souls catch up—
we left a lot of blood, but not enough. . . .
On the floodlit stage in Mexico, in heaven,
our Goddess is the Gold Coast black dancing
to Beethoven's *Ninth* in a sea of ebbing gold,
one bosom a hollow, the other a plum, she says
with stubborn shyness, 'I appreciate
your cooperation with my shortcomings. . . .
I wish on you the love of God, and a friend;
I never met a woman I could not make.' "

9. Sappho

"I set this man above the gods and heroes—
all day he sits before me face to face,
like a cardplayer. My elbow brushes his elbow;
if I should speak, he hears. The touched heart stirs,
the laughter is water hurrying over pebbles. . . .
He is the fairest thing on this dark earth;
I hear him, a hollowness is in my ears,
his footstep. I cannot speak, I cannot see.
A dead whiteness trickles pinpricks of sweat;
I am greener than the greenest green grass;
I can easily make you understand this—
a woman seldom comes to what is best:
her child, her slaves, her simple household ache—
the moon slides west; time gone; I sleep alone."

10. Antony

The righteous rioters once meant revelers,
and had the ear and patronage of kings,
for if the king were Antony, he gave
police protection, and never lost a servant.
If at daybreak he stumbled from heaven to his bed,
next day he bore his winehead like old wine;
yet would notice the fleece of the cirrus, gold, distant,
maidenhair burned in heaven's blue nausée;
then knew he lacked all substance: "If I could cure
by the Nile's green slot, a page of green papyrus;
I'll taste, God willing, the fruit of the vine no more,
nor Cleopatra, nor the thirsts of sleep."
"You'd drink the Nile to desert," she thinks. "If God
did not exist, this prayer would prove He did."

11. *A Moment*

(PAOLO AND FRANCESCA)

And she to me, "What sorrow is greater to us
than thinking in misery of the sweet time?
If you will know the first root of our love,
I'll speak as one who must both speak and weep.
On that day we were reading for dalliance
of Lancelot, and how love brought him down;
we were alone there and without suspicion,
often something read made our eyes meet,
and we blushed. A single moment destroyed us: reading
how her loved smile was kissed by such a lover.
This one who never will be divided from me
came shaking to me and kissed my trembling mouth.
That book and he who wrote it was a bawd
a Galahalt. That day we read no further."

12. *Wind*

The night blowing on this hospital is human,
Francesca's strife and monotony blown
by the folly of Christendom that loathed her flesh—
seed winds, the youthful breath of the old world,
when each progression of our carnal pleasure
was a firm extension of the soul,
the mammoth mammaries of Aphrodite.
The girl has been rowing her boat since early morning,
her jewelry is twenty wolf teeth pendant.
The snail, a dewdrop, stumbles like the blind,
puts out her little horns to test the sun—
hard riding has never blistered her agile thigh.
This whirlwind, this delirium of Eros—
winds fed the fire, a wind can blow it out.

(95)

Power

1. *Allah*

Like Henry VIII, Mohammed got religion
in the dangerous years, and smashed the celibates,
haters of life, though never takers of lives.
Changed their monasteries to iron-works,
changed their non-activist Buddhistic rote
to his clans' strict laws of *schrecklichkeit* and honor.
The Pope still twangs the harp of chastity;
the boys of the jihad rush paradise
on horseback, roam gardens stocked with adolescent
beauties, both sexes for simple nomad tastes—
how ardently they sleep in golden alcoves,
love always renewed, and the air a rose;
woman wants man, man woman, as naturally
as the thirsty frog desires the rain.

2. *Attila*

Hitler had fingertips of apprehension,
"Who knows how long I'll live? Let us have the war.
We *are* the barbarians, the world is near the end."
Attila mounted on raw meat and greens
galloped to massacre in his single fieldmouse suit,
he never entered a house that wasn't burning,
could only sleep on horseback, sinking deep
in his rural dream. Would he have found himself
in this coarsest, cruelest, least magnanimous,
most systematic, most philosophical . . .
this sedentary nomad, the "He who has, has";
who wondered why the ancient world collapsed,
then also left his festering fume of refuse,
old tins, dead vermin, ashes, eggshells, youth?

3. *Clytemnestra*

No folly can secularize the sacred cow,
our Queen at sixty worked in bed like Balzac.
Once sun and moon lay hidden in the cornstalk,
wherever she moved she left the indelible sunset,
she ruled Argos with Pharaoh's beard and beak,
the lower jaw of a waterbuffalo,
the weak intelligence, the iron will.
In one night boys fell ageless from her arms . . .
Later, something unsavory took place:
Orestes, the lord of murder and proportion,
saw that the tips of her nipples had touched her toes—
a population problem and bad art.
He knew the monster must be guillotined.
Orestes knew that Trojan chivalry was shit.

4. *The Death of Count Roland*

King Marsiliun in Saragossa
does not love God, he strides to the shade of his orchard,
he sits reclining on his bench of blue tile,
with more than twenty thousand men about him;
his speech is only the one all kings make,
it did to spark the Franco-Moorish War. . . .
At war's-end, Roland's brains seep from his ears;
he calls for the Angel Gabriel, his ivory horn,
prays for his peers, and scythes his sword, Durendal—
farther away than a man might shoot a crossbow,
toward Saragossa, there is a grassy place,
Roland goes to it, climbs the little mound:
a beautiful tree there, four great stones of marble—
on the green grass, he has fallen back, has fainted.

(97)

5. *Tamerlane Old*

To wake some midnight, on that instant senile,
clasping clay knees . . . in such warlike posture
found by your grandsons, a sheeted, shivering mound,
pressed race car hideously scared, agog with headlight,
professor in glasses—this is Timur watching
his pyramid of ninety thousand heads,
not skulls these human heads still fresh as flowers—
an architect to make Vitruvius age.
A thing well done, even a pile of heads
modestly planned to wilt before the builder,
is art, if art is everything wrung from nature . . .
We weep for the courage incurable not the victims.
The holidays in his book are mostly massacre—
fealty affirmed when friendship is a myth.

6. *Bosworth Field*

In a minute, two inches of rain stream through two flat
garden stones, clear as crystal, without trout;
we have gone down and down, gone the wrong brook—
Richard the Third was once Dickon, Duke of Gloucester,
long arm of the realm, goddam blood royal,
terrible underpinning of what could breathe—
no wonder, we have dug him up past proof.
Think of throwing your kingdom for a crown?
He threw much more, he won no life or kingdom—
Tiberius and Stalin, they killed people they knew. . . .
What does he care for Tolstoy and Saint Bernard
pointing fingers at his polio'd body;
for the moment, he is king; he is the king
shouting: it's better to have lived, than live.

7. Charles V by Titian

But we cannot go back to Charles V
barreled in armor, more gold fleece than king;
he haws on the gristle of a Flemish word,
his upper and lower Hapsburg jaws won't meet.
The sunset he tilts at is big Venetian stuff,
the true Charles, done by Titian, never lived.
The struggle he rides offstage to is offstage.
No St. Francis, he did what Francis shied at,
gave up office, one of twenty monarchs
since Saturn to willingly make the grand refusal.
In his burgherish monastery, he learned he couldn't
even put together the wheels of a clock.
He had dreamed of the democracy of Europe,
and carried enemies with him in a cage.

8. The Army of the Duc de Nemours

"I am a Christian because I am a wanton";
not Yeats this, who warned us not to lend a high
degree of reality to the Great War.
There are wars and wars, though ours are not the high-note
on the scale of sexual delirium
running the gamut of Moses' anathemas:
wantonness, sodomy, bestiality.
The Italian mercenaries besieging Lyons
for the Duc de Nemours huzzaed great flocks
of goats before them—no billies, two thousand udders
decked up in sporty green coats trimmed with gold.
They served a sound man as a mistress. Small war,
one far distant from our army mascots;
and who remembers now what Lyons paid?

9. *Bishop Berkeley*

The Bishop's nihilism is clerical,
no one was much imperiled by his life,
except he visited Newport and was Irish,
and he was not Rimbaud or Attila,
unhinged, amused to crack the world on his skull.
He lived with quality, and thought the world
is only the perceptions we perceive. . . .
In Mexico, I met this private earthquake,
when the soil trembled in the soles of my feet;
it was only my high blood of the decline,
my river system saying: I am weak,
I am Whitman, I am Berkeley . . . all men,
bathing my feet in a tub of lukewarm water;
one foot scalds the water, one foot chills the water.

10. *Old Hickory*

Those awful figures of Yankee prehistory;
the prints were cheap once, and good faith came easy:
Stephen Decatur, spyglass screwed to raking
the cannonspout-smashed Bay of Tripoli—
still, the Mohammedan believes in war;
although we had no faith to send their souls
to heaven, we were death on piracy.
Some were democratic: primitive, high-toned
President Jackson on his hobby horse,
watermelon-slice hat and presentation sword;
he might have been the Tsar or Bolivar,
pillar of the right or pillar of the left—
Andrew Jackson, despite appearances,
stands for the gunnery that widened suffrage.

11. *Sunrise*

There's always enough sunrise in hell to gasp the breeze;
the flower of what was left grew sweeter for them,
two done people conversing with bamboo fans
as if brushing the firefall from their yard—
Admiral Onishi is still a cult to his juniors
for launching the Kamikazes; he became an osprey
by mistaking our armadas for game;
his pilots loved him to annihilation.
He chats in his garden, the sky is zigzags of fire.
One butchery is left; his wife keeps nagging.
Man and wife taste cup after cup of Scotch;
how garrulously they talk about their grandchildren,
and when the knife goes home, it goes home wrong. . . .
For eighteen hours you died with your hand in hers.

12. *F. O. Matthiessen: 1902–1950*

Matthiessen jumping from the North Station hotel,
breaking his mania barrier to despair;
a prophet to the dead Czech-student torches?
Or manslaughter? Who knows whom he might have killed,
falling bald there like a shell. I'm scared
to hit this street, or stand like Stonewall Jackson
spitting on the superhighway. I wouldn't
be murdered, or even murder, for my soul;
no one can have the face to die in war.
No sleep; my feet sock-deep in bubbling sands:
it's pleasant, the effervescence, it's my heart,
unique as most are without words;
then dies—friends, wife, child—lies frozen meat,
fast colors lost to lust and prosecution.

13. *New Year's Eve 1968*

These conquered kings pass angrily away;
the gods die flesh and spirit and last in print,
each library is some injured tyrant's home.
This year runs out in the movies, it must be written
in bad, straightforward, unscanning sentences—
mine were downtrodden, branded on backs of carbons,
lines, words, letters nailed to letters, words, lines;
the typescript looked like a Rosetta Stone.
A year's black pages. Its hero *hero demens*
immovably holding off-channel for his wreck—
ill-starred of men and crossed by their fixed stars.
The slush-ice on the east water of the Hudson
rose-heather this New Year sunset; the open channel,
bright sky, bright sky, a carbon scarred with ciphers.

April's End

1. *King David Senex*

Two or three times a night, and for a month,
we wrang the night-sweat from his shirt and sheets;
on the fortieth day, we brought him Abishag,
and he recovered, and he knew her not—
cool through the hottest summer day, and moist;
her rankness more delicate than all the flowers,
as if her urine caused the vegetation,
invisible pinpricks of the golden dew;
but later, the Monarch's well-beloved shaft
lay quaking in her haven; he thought the world
was flat, yet half the globe hung on each breast,
as two spent swimmers that did cling together;
Sion come to Israel, if they had held. . . .
This clinch is quickly broken, they were glad to break.

2. *Night-Sweat*

Work-table, litter, books and standing lamp,
plain things, my stalled equipment, the old broom—
but I am living in a tidied room,
for ten nights now I've felt the creeping damp
float over my pajamas' wilted white. . . .
Sweet salt embalms me and my head is wet,
everything streams and tells me this is right;
my life's fever is soaking in night-sweat—
one life, one writing! But the downward glide
and bias of existing wrings us dry—
always inside me is the child who died,
always inside me is his will to die—
one universe, one body . . . in this urn
the animal night-sweats of the spirit burn.

3. *Caligula*

My namesake, Little Boots, Caligula,
you disappoint me. Tell me what you saw—
Item: your body hairy, badly made,
head hairless, smoother than your marble head;
Item: eyes hollow, hollow temples, red
cheeks roughed with rouge, legs spindly, hands that leave
a clammy snail's trail on your wilting sleeve,
your hand no hand can hold . . . bald head, thin neck—
you wished the Romans had a single neck.
That was no artist's bubble. Animals
ripened for your arenas suffered less
than you when slaughtered—yours the lawlessness
of something simple that has lost its law,
my namesake, not the last Caligula.

4. *To Werner von Usslingen*

Half eggshell and half eggshell, white the glass of water;
this whiteness soaked and doubled by the water,
soft goiter croaking for a plaster-cast,
heads flayed to the bone like Leonardo's felons,
deaf heads thrust forward at me not to hear
lipping with the astuteness of the deaf.
The eggshells rub like boughs. This double thing
more wizened than my skull, it isn't me—
I I; I more than I or I will die,
remembered as a plaster-cast's first cause . . .
Often fear, fame, fatuity will bring
self to the selves, to Werner von Usslingen,
his pure shield carved with German landsknecht French:
L'ennemi de Dieu et de merci.

(*104*)

5. *Nostalgie de la Boue*

The lines string out from nowhere, stretch to sorrow.
I think of others who were prominent,
musclers in any literary havoc,
now even lost to malice. "They exist,"
as the old Stalinist luminary said of friends
assigned Siberia. "It's thus," he smiled, "and thus."
Sometimes for days I only hear one voice,
one shirt that lasts five days, and not for saving.
As a child my other wife climbed a chair to dress;
"It was easier." It's easier to miss food,
not brush my teeth, forget to open mail;
the Muse shouts like vacation in my ear:
nostalgie de la boue that shelters ape
and protozoa from the rights of man.

Eloges to the Spirits

1. Revenants

They come back sometimes, we know they do,
freed like felons on the opening days of May;
if there's a healthy bite in the south wind,
Spring an echo of heaven's single day,
they sun naked like earthworms on the puddly mall.
They are better equipped for everything than people,
except perhaps for living. If we met them
covertly enough, I think we could name them all:
Cousin So, Ancestral Mother-in-Law So . . .
but we cannot laugh them into smiling back;
"A shade," they say, "is more readily killed than blackmailed."
With misty bounds they scale the starry sheer,
stare blood-eyed down into our poignant dog-yap—
as little wanting our dust as we want theirs.

2. Verdun

I bow down to the great goiter of Verdun,
and know what's waiting, ivory telephone,
ribs, hips, the pale machine-gun bleached to parchment;
they lie fatigued from too much punishment,
hang by a string to friends they knew first-hand,
to the God of our fathers still twenty, like ourselves.
Our overseas rosettes have kept their bloom,
I'm youth; since only living means to age.
I see the town we came from, twelve streets of brownstone,
cleft by a rectilinear central garden,
a formal gesture and a slice of life.
The city says, "I am the finest city!
Prague 1910." Their prince is gone a-hunting . . .
the proletariat bilingual like Verdun.

(*106*)

3. *Hydrotherapy*

No beer or washrag, half the lightbulbs busts,
still the dump was free and a gift for a king—
its rows of tubs like church-pews, infinite,
on each a reading-board, a pair of glasses,
a cake of scouring soap and Proust in French—
the men and women indistinguishable,
each breast, as the sons of Belial dreamed, a chest;
our groins are pure and fit to bear a church.
We look like our backs. We, who have been wet and cold,
soak, and for the first time in our lives are dry.
But Adam's gums still leave blood on the apple;
we can't be all things, bask in this spit of the snake,
then gaze with the naked candor of the Tsar,
his slightly bald Medusa's pewter eye.

4. *Words for a Guinea-Pig*

"Of late they leave the light on by my entry,
so I won't scare, though I never scare in the dark;
I bless this arrow that flies from wall to window—
five years and a nightlight given me to breathe;
Heidegger said that time is ecstasy . . .
I was not scared, although my life was short,
my sickly breathing the friendly sigh of leather.
Mrs. Muffin! It clicks. I had my day.
They will paint me like Cromwell with all my warts:
small mop with a tumor and eyes too popped for thought;
I was a rhinoceros when jumped by my sons.
I ate and bred, and then I only ate,
a life that reached its zenith in the 'sixties—
this short pound God threw on the scales, found wanting."

For Norman Mailer

The 9 A.M. man on the street is new,
and still the many, and he moves; he moves
in one direction for Fifth Avenue,
and up Fifth Avenue, simplex as the pigeons,
as crocked with project; but his heart is a watch,
imagines being paid for being on time.
In Buenos Aires, everyman struts the clock
twenty-four hours a day; they stride for London,
six inches taller than the best bred man:
cocks of the new order, the Nordic Cop;
they always walk straight; just as Norman Mailer's
wardrobe is two identical straight blue suits,
and two blue vests to prove monotony—
the many false faces, we single out as one.

May

1. *The Pacification of Columbia*

A patch of tan, a blood-warm roof-tile, then tan
patch, then sky patch, as the jigsaw flung some mosque of Omar
to vaultless consummation and blue consumption,
exhalation of the sands of the desert to fire.
I got the message, one the puzzle never sent. . . .
No destructive element emaciates
Columbia this Mayday afternoon;
the thickened buildings look like buildings out
of Raphael, colossal classic, dungeon feudal;
horses, higher artistic types than their grooms,
forage Broadway's median trees, as if
nature were liberated . . . the police
lean on the burnished, nervous hides, show they,
at least, have learned to meet and reason together.

May 1, 1968

2. *Violence*

From the first cave, the first farm, the first sage,
inalienable our human right to murder—
"We must get used," they say, "to the thought of guns;
we must get used to seeing guns; we must
get used to using guns." Guns too are mortal. Guns
failed Che Guevara, Marie Antoinette,
Leon Trotsky, the children of the Tsar:
chivalrous ornaments to power. Tom Paine said
Burke pitied the plumage and forgot the dying bird.
How can a plucked bird live? Whoever puts
arms in the hands of the people is a criminal,
arms given the people are always used against the people;
the only guns that will not kill the owner
are forged by insight . . . fear made wise by anger.

(*109*)

3. *Leader of the Left*

Love will not blame it on his blind ambition,
or blinder courage (both sowed their dirty germs)
or some ostracizing glandular unbalance;
it was his miracle that closed his eyes,
when his whole face took on a flesh of wood,
slab of raw plastic grafted to his one
natural feature, scars from the demonstrations,
he bore like a Heidelberg student for the New Left.
His voice, electric, was a low current whir;
by now he'd bypassed sense and even eloquence;
without listening, the audience understood;
anticipating the sentence, they too swayed
to the predestined poignance of his murder,
his Machiavellian Utopia of pure nerve.

4. *The Restoration*

The old king enters his study with the police;
it's much like mine left in my hands a month:
unopened letters, the thousand cigarettes,
open books, yogurt cups in the unmade bed—
the old king enters his study with the police,
but all in all, his study is much worse than mine;
an edge of malice puts the seal of man:
frames smashed, their honorary honors lost,
all the unopened letters have been answered.
He halts at woman-things that can't be his,
he says, "To think that human beings did this!"
The sergeant picks up a defiled *White Goddess,* or is it
Secret Memoirs of the Courts of Europe?
"Would a human beings do this things to these book?"

5. De Gaulle

Seldom fine virtue without true words; yet he
who dumbly guns his government on virtue
is like the northern star, which keeps its place,
which keeps its place, and all the stars turn to it;
asks faithfulness and sincerity, though these
do more for usurpers than the tyranny;
while he, unseeing, says: a true man acts,
then speaks, speaks in accordance with his act:
what is good for the swarm is good for the bee—
learning without thought is labor lost;
and thought without learning? It is perilous;
as if law could be the fulfillment of love,
as if freedom is to be invisible,
piss in any direction on your lawn.

6. The Ark

Time gone, when we enjoyed perverse harangues,
and hit the scientists with Plato's corkscrew—
youth! Ours advanced an art as disciplined
and dark as Calvin in his *Institutes,*
our faith was meter; Greece built the final theater—
but now there're no takers for this argument. . . .
Two buildings, two futures, go up across my street;
one at Harvard, the other in New York;
one churns at six, the other at six-thirty,
but best the men shouting on the wooden ribs—
thus on the ribs of the Ark and in his cups,
Noah harangued the world he wished to save. . . .
How could the reckless, authoritative young
bear us, if we were given length of days?

7. *The New York Intellectual*

How often was this last salute recast?
Did the old critic need three hundred words,
such tact and tough, ascetic resonance,
the preposition *for,* five times in parallel,
to find himself "a beleaguered minority,
without fantasies of martyrdom,"
facing the graves of the New York Intellectuals,
"without joy, but neither with dismay"?
This art was needed for his quiet message,
his firm and unpermissive final sentence.
How often one would choose the poorman's provincial
out of town West Side intellectual
for the great brazen rhetorician serpent,
swimming the current with his iron smile!

8. *The Dissenting Academy*

The Moslem's hack-moon hangs over WABC
TELEVISION, with its queue of stand-ins;
real trees, the sky-distempered, skim of winter,
tremble on a yellow, nondescript brick tower—
our city! No garden city curbs more poodles,
our iron grinds like a hundred kinds of birds;
that's us, it isn't worth writing home about,
this is our home. . . . The scholar escapes his time;
college ivy darkens his small-pane window,
leaves gross as grapeleaf. His students prime the pump,
till he wattles like a turkey to his grant.
Scholarship proves the scholar less than mortal;
why should anyone settle for New York?
Dying without death is a life in the city.

9. *The Doctor*

We know what orthodox analysis
could do with her, the talented, the taloned
cat hooked on the cold fish of Abelard.
They had one soul once, though his brain is bone,
and her neglected ember is extinct.
After his prison, to the woman came
energy such as she never knew before,
sprinkling on us like a fresh flow of blood,
old Sorbonne argot, filth for Saint Bernard,
untimely, mystical, pledged to the police. . . .
Abelard's tortuous debater's points
flew to the mark, feathered with her ecstasy—
his student crushes, and his fall like lightning,
in love with the dialectic, his Minerva. . . .

10. *Another Doctor*

"Have you ever lost a year off . . . somewhere?
The new owner can't sell it back to us, can he?
Our terrible losses, Harry Truman's loss
of a minute's sleep for Hiroshima, less than
a boy catching the paw of his mutt in the door of a car . . .
We're ghosts . . . Twice I heard a rattling stress of cherrystones,
then by my bed, a man. That flight was feudal
on steel-capped hoof and wing and foot of blood.
I've killed worse dragons—my doctor's on Heidegger
in German, in Germany, for my German Prof.
I love Lenin, he was so feudal. 'When I listen to Beethoven,'
he said, 'I think of stroking people's hair;
what we need are people to chop the head off.'
The horizontal is blood-colored and made by man."

11. *New York*

We must have had a lift once from New York
thirty years back, or two; it's hard to think,
gone like Sunday mahjong and netting butterflies—
someone comes here from the outlands, Trinidad,
tuned to another metropolis, Port of Spain;
deplanes here, knowing no one, strapped, thirsty
to hoof the streets of wonder. . . . Each plateglass
display looks a nightclub from a block away,
each nightclub Islam with its liveried tariff,
all the money, all the connection. . . . One has none,
triggered for the liberated girl with a build,
Prometheus, bayoneted at the barricade,
thrills to the King of Prussia's war-cheer, "Advance,
you bastards, do you want to live forever?"

12. *Sounds in the Night*

Nothing new in them yet their old roles startle;
asked to adapt, they swear they cannot swerve:
machines our only friends who live to serve us,
metal, mortal and mechanical,
their dissonance varied as our northern birds—
clean and singing through the night air dirt!
Sleepless I drink their love, if it is love.
Miles below heaven, luminous in some courtyard,
dungeoned by primitive wall-brick windowless,
the grass conservative cry of the cat in heat—
"Who cares if the running stream is sometimes stopped?
Inexhaustible the springs from which I flow."
Cats will be here when man is prehistory,
man doomed to outlast the body of his work.

13. *Civilization*

Your skirt stopped half a foot above my knee,
personal birthmarks varied your black mesh,
and yet I praise your legs as generic legs—
and who would want to finger or approach
what ruminated through your printed sweater?
Civilization will always outrun life,
its toleration means to bear and ache,
hurt, hate oneself, as no one wants to twice.
That's Locke, that's Mill; the Liberal lies with that,
sucks his own blood to bare his icy tooth;
that's why there are none, that's why we are none,
why the worst bastard shivers once a moon,
if the god Eros arcs into the Virgin;
as you, no virgin, made me bear myself.

14. *The Diamond Cutters*

That terrible late October summer day;
we passed the diamond cutters and appraisers,
hole-in-the-corners on 47th Street—
trade ancient as the Ur-kings' bank-account,
the loss of empire for a grain of dust;
all was in essence, rare and hard and bright.
Herman Melville would have had the meaning,
while gritting his final dogdays in New York,
far from his cousin dogfish and white whale;
but no one can avoid the thoughts of man:
mason's chisel on the throat of a stone. . . .
We were boulevarding out the time till lunch;
the conversation was inaudible to You,
eye brighter than the uncut sun at noon.

(115)

15. *The Picture*

(FOR ELIZABETH)

This might be nature—twenty stories high,
two water tanks, tobacco shingle, girdled
by stapled pasture wire, while bed to bed,
we lie gazing into the ether's crystal ball,
sky and a sky and sky and sky, till death—
my heart stops, this might be heaven. Twenty years
ago, we shot for less, could settle for
a picture, out of style then and now in,
of seven daffodils. We watched them blow:
buttercup yellow were the flowers, and green
the stems as fresh paint, over them the wind,
the blowzy wooden branches of the elms,
the sack of hornets sopping up the flame—
still over us, still in parenthesis.

16. *Lunch Date*

Mullioned windows of a Madison Avenue British pub,
one's astream with noonday, the other sundown,
streams on the grander glass of a sporting print:
Old England tarted up with boor and barmaid,
her color roused and rouged by horsier custom,
as a reflection elevates the coarse.
Often color lines are dulled and blurred
in the great city, most of all, this more exotic.
I touch your lifeline; no one is disarmed,
or handcuffed. It's not malevolence but inertia
gives men the legs to meet their obligations.
Can the artist or man see without active sloth?
Two windows, one reflection, a bypasser
passing the windows; he divides to meet.

17. *Memorial Day*

Sometimes I sink a thousand centuries,
bone tired or stone asleep, to sleep ten seconds—
voices, their future voices, adolescents,
go crowding through the chilling open windows:
fathomless profundities of inanimation.
And we will be, then, and as they are here.
But nothing will be put back right in time,
done over, thought through straight again—not my father
revitalizing in a simple Rhineland spa,
Mussolini's misguiding roosterstep
in the war year, just before *our* War began. . . .
Ah, ah, this house of twenty-foot apartments,
all the windows yawning—the voices of its tutees,
their fortissimo *Figaro,* sunk into dead brick.

Robert Kennedy: 1925–1968

1. R.F.K.

Here in my workroom, in its listlessness
of Vacancy, some old Victorian house,
airtight and sheeted for old summers,
far from the hornet yatter of the bond—
is loneliness, a thin smoke thread of vital
air. What can I catch from you now?
Doom was woven in your nerves, your shirt,
woven in the great clan; they too were loyal,
and you too more than loyal to them, to death.
For them like a prince, you daily left your tower
to walk through dirt in your best cloth. Untouched,
alone in my Plutarchan bubble, I miss
you, you out of Plutarch, made by hand—
forever approaching our maturity.

2. *Another Circle*

The modulation is most alive and firm,
when three or four colors are about the same,
when three or four words sound much the same,
say much the same. That's hardly how we talk
this first ride of summer, Harriet: I trapped in words,
you gagging your head-over-heels articulation.
The search. The circle. We can't hunt God. He hunts us,
and his story is sad . . . the Irish in black, three rows
ranked for the future photograph, the Holy Name,
fiercely believed in then, then later held to
perhaps more fiercely in their unbelief.
How they hated to leave this unpremeditated
gesture of their life! No Name can judge their killer,
his guiltless liver, kidneys, fingertips and phallus.

3. *Another June*

Nervous leaves twitter on the high wood tree,
this and that thing, grape-purple, skims the lawn,
night shrouds the monopolies of Rome and Carthage,
the oil is spent, the oilpumps seesaw thirst.
Who can believe the nesting, sexing tree swallow
would dive for an eye or brain . . . this handbreadth insect,
navy butterfly, the harbinger of rain,
change to danger in this twilight? Will we
swat out the birds as ruthlessly as flies? . . .
One was refreshed when you wisecracked through the guests,
usually somewhat woodenly, hoarsely dry,
pure Celt on the eastern seaboard. Who was worse stranded?
Is night only your torchlight wards gone black,
wake written on the waves, pyre set for the fire that fell?

To Summer

1. *The Worst Sinner*

The earliest sportsman in our earliest dawn,
waking to what redness, waking a killer,
saw the red cane was sweet in his red grip;
the blood of the sheep matched the blood of the wolf;
yet Jonathan Edwards learned how to think himself
worse than any man that ever breathed;
he was a good man, and he thought with reason—
which of us hasn't thought the same thought worse?
Each night I lie me down to sleep in rest;
two or three times a week, I wake to my sin—
sins, not sin; not two or three days, seven.
God himself cannot wake up five years younger,
and drink away the chalice of our death-sentence,
like the best man in the best possible world.

2. *God of Our Fathers*

Say it's the one-way trip, the one-way flight,
strip the worse meaning from *trip* and *flight;*
then you could say you stood in the cold light of science,
seeing as you are seen, espoused to fact.
Strange, a life is the fire and fuel; we,
the animals, the objects, must be here
without a title-deed of evidence
that anything that ever stopped living
ever falls back to living when life stops.
There's more romance to the watchmaker God
of Descartes and Paley; He drafted and installed
the Apparatus for us. He loved to tinker—
Who having perfected what He had to do,
stood off shrouded in his loneliness.

(120)

3. *Whites*

This summer night, and then the summer night,
windows reflecting lighted on that white—
the door between is not the door between:
the Sabines, Casanova's weeping willow,
Death dropping his marble scythe to be a brother,
one skeleton among the skeletons. . . .
Ghengis and Attila killed fewer of their kind.
This kind is only expelled by prayer and fasting;
yet we were no kinder when we had the Faith,
and thought the massacred could be reformed,
and move like angels in the unwithering white,
file upon file, the beds of long-neck clams,
blue-white and hard and sharp and stiff and pure—
the clam-shell cunted in the ground of being.

4. *Heaven*

Smoke weakens the dim greens of Mexico,
the City, not the nation; as if field fires
of marijuana fumed in the back yards.
One sees the green dust as the end of life;
and through it, heaven. . . . Some child or cubist flays
the gardens of Versailles to cube, cone and ball—
this shouldn't strain our imagination. Heaven,
if we can be there, must be perfect. I've been there,
seen the Sun-King spit into the wind of Versailles;
he cannot tell his left hand from his right,
he holds up two smooth stones, marked *left* and *right*. . . .
In the straight hall, the straighter curtains lift,
a head higher, two heads higher, than the old dead King;
they dance spontaneously in the atheist air.

5. *The House-Party*

(FOR LOUIS MACNEICE, 1907–1963)

Two dozen children would visit half a dozen;
downstairs the lost child bullied the piano,
getting from note to note like jumping ties;
the black keys showed their bruises and turned white.
The games he heard outside and missed were no
less crudely commonplace and soundly crude—
but no need to be Bach to be what we are . . .
First when watching his father, the Bishop, wade
up-trout-stream barefoot, he liked him, "What poor feet!"
"Until I was almost thirty," he said, "I thought
a woman would roll on me, and smother me."
A month from his death, we stood by Epstein's bust
of Bertrand Russell; Louis said, "It's better
to die at fifty than lose our pleasure in terror."

6. *For Theodore Roethke: 1908–1963*

At Yaddo, you shared a bathroom with a bag
tree-painter whose boobs bounced in the basin,
your blues basin where you wished to plunge your head. . . .
All night, my friend, no friend, you swam my sleep;
this morning you are lost in the Maine sky,
close, cold and gray, smoke, smoke-colored cloud.
Sheeplike, unsociable, reptilian, the shags
fly in straight lines like duck in a shooting booth,
divers winning to the darker monochrome.
You honored nature, helpless, elemental
creature, and touched the waters of the offing;
you left them quickened with your name: Ted Roethke. . . .
Omnipresent, the Mother made you nonexistent,
you, the ocean's anchor, our high tide.

7. *For Eugene McCarthy*

I love you so. . . . Gone? Who will swear you wouldn't
have done good to the country, that fulfillment wouldn't
have done good to you—the father, as Freud says:
you? We've so little faith that anyone
ever makes anything better—the same and less—
or that ambition ever makes the ambitious;
the state lifts us, we cannot change the state—all
was yours though, lining down the balls for hours,
freedom in the hollow bowling-alley:
crack of the globe, the boys. . . . Picking a quarrel
with you is like picking the petals of the daisies—
the game, the passing crowds, the rapid young
still brand your hand with sunflecks . . . coldly willing
to smash the ball past those who bought the park.

July 6, 1968

8. *The Immortals*

"Dear Mary, with her usual motherly
solicitude for the lost overdog. . . ."
You've always wished to stand by a white horse,
a Jeanne d'Arc by Albrecht Dürer, armed and lettered
in the tougher university of the world. . . .
Since your travels, the horse is firmly there;
you stare off airily into the mundane gossip,
our still more mundane ethics, listen puzzled,
take note; once or twice, blurt your ice-clear sentence—
one hand, for solace, braided in the horse's mane. . . .
The immortals are all about us and below us;
for us *immortal* means another book;
there are too many . . . with us, the music stops;
the first violin stops to wipe the sweat from his bow.

(*123*)

9. *For Harpo Marx*

Harpo Marx, your hand white-feathered the harp—
the only words you ever spoke were sound.
The movie's not always the sick man of the arts,
yours touched the stars; Harpo, your changing picture
is an unchanging still life, not nature dead.
You dumbly memorized an unwritten script . . .
I saw you first two years before you died,
near Fifth in Central Park, in fragile autumn:
old blond hair too blonder, old eyes too young.
Two movie trucks and five police lay spoke-wheel
like the covered wagon. The crowd as much or little.
I wish I had knelt; I age to your wincing smile—
Dante's movies, his groups of pain and motion;
the genus *happy* is one generic actor.

10. *Milton in Separation*

It was no loss to the cool and Christian Homer,
blind, cradled in his chair of work, pronouncing
divorce and *marriage* with hard, sardonic R's.
Though the dawn of separation was blank as any,
he only cared for life in the straits. Her flight
put a live elbow in his marble Eve. At first,
she filled the thirst for emptiness;
they grappled, then fell hookloose from the fireflesh . . .
Live-cold in some Greenland on the globe's eyebrow,
free now to study what wooed you most, your writing,
your overobsession posterity must pay.
The bare skim milk of your study is blue to blindness;
the goldfinch flame in the tinderbush. You wished
to set the woods on fire and melt the glacier.

11. *Stalin*

Winds on the stems make them creak like things made by man;
a hedge of vines and bushes—three or four
kinds, grape leaf, elephant ear and alder,
an arabesque, imperfect and alive,
a hundred hues of green, the darkest shades
short of black, the palest leaf-backs far from white.
The state, if we could see behind the walls,
is woven of perishable vegetation.
Stalin? What shot him clawing up the tree of power—
millions plowed under like the crops they grew,
his intimates dying like the spider-bridegroom?
The large stomach could only chew success. What raised him
was the usual lust to break the icon,
joke cruelly, seriously, and be himself.

Eight Months Later

1. *Eight Months Later*

It's certain we burned the grass, the grass now burning:
the dismal stones of the field make off for the pond;
safe in the muddy water, they change to ducks
in brown fatigues, eight ducks without a drake—
if we lose the war eight women without a man. . . .
The cement mixer sings like a choir of locusts.
The worst of Manhattan is everything is stacked:
ten buildings dancing in the hat of one,
some rugged, one-family, 1890's château.
One family? This would house the early Mormons,
their *droit de seigneur*. One cell would tent Mohammed
through the teat-blown sand. . . . I wish I were elsewhere;
Mexico . . . Mexico? Where is Mexico?
Who will live this year back, cat on the ladder?

2. *Die Gold-Orangen*

We see the country where the lemon blossoms,
and the pig-gold orange glows on its dark branch,
and the south wind stutters from the blue hustings;
the bluebell is brown, the cypress points too straight—
we see it; it's behind us, love, behind us.
Do you see the house, the roof on marble pillars?
The sideboard silvers, and the arbors blaze;
the statue stands naked to stare at you.
What have I done with us, and what was done?
And the mountain, El Volcán, the climb of clouds?
The mule-man lost his footing in the clouds,
seed of the dragon coupled in the caves. . . .
The cliff drops; over it, the water drops,
and steams away the marks that led us on.

We Do What We Are

1. *The Nihilist as Hero*

"All our French poets can turn an inspired line,
but which has written six passable in sequence?"
said Valéry. That was a happy day for Satan . . .
One wants words meat-hooked from the living steer—
but the cold flame of tinfoil licks the metal log,
it's the beautifully unchanging fire of childhood;
it betrays monotony of vision.
Life by definition must breed on change,
each season we scrap old cars and wars and women.
But sometimes when I am ill or delicate,
the pinched flame of my match turns living green,
the cornstalk in green tails and seeded tassel . . .
Only a nihilist desires the world
to be as it is, or much more passable.

2. *Grave Guild*

Six poets at a table in the Plaza's ball-and-game-room,
bright as a Viking ship the Dark Age shields,
a forged, eclectic conglomerate of our dreams.
Six hands on the dusty bust of the microphone—
So Charlemagne loved his three R's and feared for the future,
when he saw the first Normans float out from the Rhine.
Six skulls, the best minds of my generation,
coiffures as out of style as what we write;
six hands on the dusty bust of the microphone:
"Read us your great collage, or something old,
since nothing dead is alien to our tongue."
O Weathercock made to face both ways! I read;
by some oversight not a word is I—
two O's for eyes in an O for the face of an I . . .

3. In the Back Stacks

(PUBLICATION DAY)
My lines swell up and spank like the bow of a yacht;
outside, the break-up of the Broadway bookstores,
outside, the higher voltage of *studenten*,
the revolution seeking her professor . . .
It's life in death to be bound, delivered, published,
lie on reserve like the old Boston *British Poets*—
hanged for keeping meter? They were complete with Keats;
the editor saw no necessity for America,
tongue dead as the Latin of the Americas . . .
One talked such junk all summer behind the stacks.
Things happened when we were talked out, or the sun went out,
lay incommunicado . . . The anthology holds up
without us, the gasp in Cleopatra's gap—
everything printed will come to these back stacks.

May 19, 1969

4. Reading Myself

Like millions, I took just pride and more than just,
first striking matches that brought my blood to boiling;
I memorized tricks to set the river on fire,
somehow never wrote something to go back to.
Even suppose I had finished with wax flowers
and earned a pass to the minor slopes of Parnassus . . .
No honeycomb is built without a bee
adding circle to circle, cell to cell,
the wax and honey of a mausoleum—
this round dome proves its maker is alive,
the corpse of such insect lives preserved in honey,
prays that the perishable work live long
enough for the sweet-tooth bear to desecrate—
this open book . . . my open coffin.

Circles

1. *Homing*

(FOR ELIZABETH)
To our 20th. We stand set: two trees, their roots;
sometimes the greenest cracks soonest in this soil,
white shells and sinking sand. One form *per sempre;*
ten or fifteen pounds superior, since
the Graces gave their hard gold ring, their fistcuff, *Love*—
crown met by what bypaths! Things cling to the aging:
Pharaoh, now black shellac, has the hair of a squaw,
orchid smelling purer than the live green grass.
By setting limits, man has withdrawn from the monsters:
metal rods and then another metal rod;
true markers mark-step, they neither take nor give.
And when I show my head by your birdhouse, you dive me,
graceful, higher, quicker . . . unsteady swallow. . . .
Who will uproot the truth that cannot change?

2. *The Hard Way*

(FOR HARRIET)
Don't hate your parents, or your children will hire
unknown men to bury you at your own expense.
Child, as old as your mother or father, last-year-high—
who will see the coruscations of your furrow,
adolescence sharking up salt mullet,
your destiny written in our hands rewritten?
Under the stars, one sleeps then, freed from household,
tufts of grass and dust and tufts of grass,
night oriented to the star of youth—
tough as the she-wolf's tits that suckled Rome,
per aspera ad astra. In backward Maine,
ice goes in season to the tropical,
then the mash freezes back to ice, and then
the ice is broken by another wave.

3. *Das ewig Weibliche*

Serfs with a finer body and tinier brain—
who asks the swallows to do drudgery,
clean, cook, peck up their ton of dust per diem?
Knock on their homes, they go up tight with fear,
farting about all morning past their young,
small as wasps fuming in their ash-leaf ball.
Nature lives off the life that comes to hand;
yet if we knew and softly felt their being,
wasp, bee and bird might live with us on air;
the boiling yellow-jacket in her sack
of zebra-stripe cut short above the knee
escape . . . the nerve-wrung creatures, wasp, bee and bird,
felons for life or keepers of the cell,
wives in their wooden cribs of seed and feed.

4. *Sound Mind, Sound Body*

Mens sana? O at last; from twenty years
of the annual mania, thirty of adolescence:
this crown. And I am still *in corpore sano?*
Some mornings now my studies wane by eleven,
afternoons by three. The print, its brain,
clouds in mid-chapter, just as I will go—
two score and ten . . . less than common expectation?
All the new years turned in for old? Old times,
when death was nothing, death the dirty crown
on a sound fingernail—ephemeral,
though avant-garde? Now I can tan on my belly
without impatience, almost hear out old people,
live off the family chronicle—the swallow
scents out the kinship, dares swoop me from her nest.

5. Penelope

Manet's bourgeois husband takes the tiller at Cannes,
the sea is right, the virgin's cocky boater,
naïve as the moon, streams with its heartstring ribbons—
as if Ulysses were a Sunday friendship. . . .
"Do clothes make the man, or a man the clothes?"
he whistles, gets no answer, sees the household
include him in its polished hollowness,
cellar, womb and the growths—this master, able
to change a silk purse into a sow's ear,
marching his knife-bright floors for wolftracks, thinking
something like this, or something not like this:
"How many a brave heart broken on monologue
revives on ass, or turns to alcohol.
Is it silk cuts scissors, or scissors silk?"

6. Struggle of Non-Existence

Here on this bank where Darwin found his fair one,
and thirty kinds of weeds of the wood in flower,
and a blue shirt, a blue shirt, and our love-beads
rattling together to show that we were young—
we found the fume-gray thistle far-gone in flower.
God dwells inside us and the plowman worm
working this soil that must have lost much sweetness
when Eden and the funk of Abel taught man
the one thing worse than war is massacre . . .
Man turns to dimwit quicker than the mayfly,
asks lucid moments, sleepless drowsiness;
the tissue sings to sinew, "Passerby . . ."
Dying beside you, I feel the live blood simmer
in my palms and my feet, and know I am alive.

7. *The Spock etc. Sentences*

The black hardrubber bathtub stoppers at the Parker House
must have been ordered for their Majesties,
William IV and George IV, then tailored
to the tastes and weight of William Howard Taft.
Things were made right in those days—24-carat
sky over Boston and our first steps to jail.
All night we slept to the sawing of immense
machines constructing: saws in circles slicing
white crescents, shafts and blocks, as if the scheming
intellectuals had rebuilt Tyre and Sidon *ab ovo*—
far from our treasonable, reasonable taunts to save the country,
soft conventions of discourse with lawyers, judge and jury;
"We have had all we can have, and have ruined
so much we cannot safely ruin this."

July 10, 1968

8. *The Good Life*

To see the trees flower, and leaves pearl with mist,
fan out above us on the wineglass elms,
life's frills and the pith of life: wife, child and house;
decomposition burning out in service . . .
ass-licking for medals on the peacock lawn,
tossing the birdseed to the blooded gamecock,
bellowing in the purple bullring of the slave—
the Rome of Spartacus, dull, martyred and anxious to please.
Fresh legions and old religions hold the winning.
One goes on wondering though, how the imperial tackle,
seldom pleasant and a flail of gallstone,
draws to something otherwise forgotten,
the sleeping dog, the hero hired for terror,
pearls for the necklace, teeth for the clinking chain.

(*132*)

9. *Night Worms*

Tree-worms beam bright white gray in the night;
inside a truck-shed, old tires are hung like paintings. . . .
We say, "Everyone accepts our claim to greatness,
our best photographers dare not face us.
If blood doesn't spurt from our eyelashes, when we meet
a work of art, it isn't art." In schemes,
too far is easy, enough a miracle;
yet God is good, he sees us all as straw dogs.
Even the toothless, trodden worm can writhe—
in the night-moment, even the halt-pacifist,
nursed on straws and wheat-germ, hears the drum-step
of his kind whistle like geese in converging lines,
hears the police weep in their fog of Mace,
while he plants the black flag of anarchy and peace.

10. *The Vogue, the Vague*

Our *New York Times Cookbook* looks like *Leaves of Grass*—
I turn the page: I have escaped its death,
take my two eggs with butter, drink and smoke.
I live past prudence. This is common good
usage. But who can drink the shifting cloud,
lie in small-talk, and tell the truth in print,
be Iago offstage, or Lincoln out of office?
The vague, the vogue, what do they tell the critic?
Beethoven's theme is Romantic, but too good:
the republic, death to kings, the living God,
Napoleon. He was his own Napoleon,
star-bound like the First to the Age of Reason.
Was the captive chorus of *Fidelio* bound?
Does the painted soldier in the painting bleed?

11. *High Blood*

I watch my blood pumped into crystal pipes,
red sticks like ladycrackers for a child—
nine-tenths of me, and yet it's lousy stuff.
Touched, it stains, slips, drips, sticks; and it's lukewarm.
All else—the brains, the bones, the stones, the soul—
is peripheral flotsam on this live flow.
On my great days of sickness, I was God;
and now I might be. I catpad on my blood,
and the universe moves beneath me when I move.
It's the aorta and heartbeat of my life;
hard rock turned high, chosen record purring,
as if the sapphire in the cat were stuck—
cry of high blood for blood that gives both tyrant
and tyrannized their short half-holiday.

12. *The Lost Tune*

As I grow older, I must admit with terror:
I have been there, the masterwork has lost;
music that taught, philosophies that danced,
their *vivace* clogs; I am too wise, or tired;
one's read the book, even the woman dies,
most women hold up longer than the arts—
yours was landscape, engraved in black and white
to better show the formal luxury of
a million trees and creepers marching up
the flank of a cliff, microscopes on each leaf;
below, your weaponed huntress hunts her huntsman,
the lover panting to her stag at bay;
not very true, yet art—had Schubert sung them, risen
from the Vienna greenroom to this death.

13. *Heat*

For the first time in fifteen years, a furnace
Maine night that would have made summer anywhere;
Arizona. The wooden rooms of our house
dry, redoubling their wooden farmhouse smell,
honest wooden ovens shaking with desire.
We feared the pressure might be too curative.
Outside, a young seal festered on the beach,
head snapped off, the color of a pig;
much lonelier, this formula for cures.
One nostril shut, my other attenuated—
it's strange tonight to want to teach and pencil
self-help on bits of paper, "I must remember
to breathe through my mouth. Breathe from your mouth,"
as the mouth kept closing on the breath of morning.

The Races

1. *August*

This night the mustard bush and goldenrod
and more unlikely yellows tread a spiral,
blue china snakes, blue ribbons—cool not cold,
the vase eviscerated down to ribbon. . . .
Brotherly, stacked and mean, the great Convention
throws out its Americana like dead flowers:
choices, at best, that cannot hurt, or cure;
many are chosen, and so few are called. . . .
And yet again, I see the yellow bush rise,
formations, I suppose, beyond the easel;
one summer, two summers, young breasts escape the rib;
the future is only standing on our feet,
and what can be is only what will be—
the sun warms the mortician, unpolluted.

August 7, 1968

2. *Five-Hour Rally*

All excel, as if they were the key-note speaker,
first of the twenty first-ballerinas in the act,
all original or at least in person . . .
This acre of carpet is coal-on-cherry sunset,
one figure to each ten feet, like the rich in his grave;
its head is a broken pretzel, less head than gulf;
the wings are fernshoots, done like ironwork
for a Goya balcony, lure and bar to love.
The belly is a big watermelon seed,
the body is the belly's overcoat—
poor vermin, it could only live for that . . .
Sunrise comes. Who can live on breath alone?
Insects and politicians grapple on the carpet,
saying, "You will swallow me. I you."

3. *The Flaw*

The old flaw in my eye is sprouting bits and strings
gliding like dragon-kites in the Chinese sky;
I was afraid to look more closely, and count—
today I am too exhausted to be afraid,
I gaze in the white-cloud window of my plane,
see in it my many flaws are still the one,
a flaw with a tail the color of shed skin,
inaudible rattle of the rattler's disks.
God is design, this ugliness confides
the goodness of His will, and gives me warning—
the scrape of the Thunderer's fingernail. . . .
Faust's soul-sale is for life to do his work;
yet death is sweet now, weariness almost lets
me taste its sweetness none will ever taste.

4. *Fear in Chicago*

The little millionaire's place, sheen of the centuries;
as my eye roved, everything freshly French;
then I saw a score marked *sans rigueur*
on the little grand piano, muddy white,
a blank white and medallion-little bust
of Franz Schubert, a blown-up colored photograph
of the owner's wife, executive-Bronzino—
this frantic touch of effort! Or out-window,
two cunning cylinder skyscraper apartment buildings—
six circles of car garage below the homes,
moored boats below the cars—more Louis Quinze
and right than anything in this apartment;
except the little girl's bedroom, perfect with posters:
"Do not enter," and "Sock it to me, Baby."

August 26, 1968

5. "We Are Here to Preserve Disorder"

The beefy door ajar an inch or two,
dead news, a roll-bed, scenes on the green screen. . . .
I saw a dark strip of silenced stalk in rippling,
the singed back of a Siamese cat that crashed my gate—
non-verbal Cordelia, the wordless voice of Chicago.
Some cats are persons . . . mine packed and left a bottle:
"R. Lowell: for nervousness, Dr. Baumann."
The police weren't baby-sitting at 5 A.M.;
in our staff headquarters, three heads smashed, one club.
Five days the Hilton was liberated with troops and cars—
a fallen government. The youth for McCarthy
knew and blew too much; their children's crusade!
Waste fell from the windows at the end of the party. . . .
"How can you have a Convention, if you can't throw out a beer-can?"

6. After the Convention

Life, hope, they conquer death, generally, always;
and if the steamroller goes over the flower, the flower dies.
Some are more solid earth; they stood in lines,
blouse and helmet, a creamy de luxe sky-blue—
their music, savage and ephemeral. . . .
After five nights of Chicago: police and mob,
I am so tired and had, clichés are wisdom,
the clichés of paranoia. On this shore,
the fall of the high tide waves is a straggling, joshing
march of soldiers . . . on the march for me. . . .
How slender and graceful, the double line of trees,
how slender, graceful, irregular and underweight,
the young in black folk-fire circles below the trees—
under their bodies, the green grass turns to hay.

September 1, 1968

7. *The Hospital*

We're lost here if we follow what we read,
worse lost if hearsay is our common voice;
we need courses in life and death and what's alive;
trips to the hospital. . . . One has seen stiffs
that look alive, they mostly look alive,
twitched by green fingers till they turn to flowers;
they are and are not—some poor candidate,
the stone-deaf ear no felon's sledge will wake—
others are strapped to their cots, thrust out in hallways,
browner, dirtier, flatter than the dead leaves,
they are whatever crinkles, plugged to tubes,
and plugged to jugs of dim blue doctored water,
held feet above them to lift their eyes to God—
these look dead, unlike the others, they are alive.

8. *Forethought*

(FOR HARRIET)

I dream a kind of camp army, not altogether
anything from Chicago, has barbwired off
my house. I wake up, shouting, "No, don't, don't!"
I seize hold of my consciousness, prove myself
but half awake, run the doubtful parallel
between human life and the moment just now gone. . . .
To live long enough to see our children live:
this has been thought before, is current slang.
You are too young to wish us otherwise,
too thoughtful ever to wish us wholly other;
though to see you happy, we would have to live
your life with you, hold hard, and live you out.
It doesn't go this way; this doesn't go—
so calm, perhaps, will be the final change.

September 4, 1968

9. *November 6*

Election Night, the last Election Night,
without drink, television or a friend—
wearing my dark blue knitted tie to classes. . . .
No one has recognized that blue meant black.
My daughter telephones me from New York,
she talks *New Statesman,* "Then we're cop-outs! Isn't
not voting Humphrey a vote for Nixon and Wallace?"
And I, "Not voting Nixon is my vote for Humphrey."
It's funny-awkward; I don't come off too well;
"You mustn't tease me, we were clubbed in Chicago."
We must rouse our broken forces and save the country:
we often said this, now the fallen angels
open old wounds and hunger for the blood-feud
hidden like contraband and loved like whiskey.

10. *November 7: From the Painter's Loft*

The slick bare tar, the same suburban station;
most of Boston is now a housing project,
sterile, clean, unspoiled. Here nothing's slid
since 1925. The Prudential Building
that raised and saved the skyline, here does nothing;
paper-weight, a removable plug-in. We can
still gulp Bohemia with the boorishness of boys
from this window, and see the *Thread and Needle Shoppe,*
where we stole a fifteen-dollar microscope,
then tried to make them pay us fifteen dollars. . . .
Nobody has won, nobody has lost;
on the broad tar, the starry headlights twinkle
from Portland, Maine to Portland, Oregon.
Will the election-winners ever pay us back?

Summer

1. *These Winds*
(FOR HARRIET)
I see these winds, these are the tops of trees,
these are no heavier than green alder bushes;
touched by a light wind, they begin to mingle
and race for instability—too well placed
to last out a day in the brush, these are the winds. . . .
Downstairs, you correct notes at the upright piano,
doubly upright this midday torn from the whole
green cloth of summer; your room is dark as a cloakroom,
the loose tap beats time, you hammer the formidable
chords of *The Nocturne,* your second composition.
Since you first began to bawl and crawl
from sheltered lawn to this shady room, how often
these winds have crossed the wind of inspiration—
in these too, the unreliable touch of the all.

2. *La Condition Humaine*
(FOR HARRIET)
Should someone human, not just our machinery
firing on its fling, do for the world and us,
surely they'll say he chose the lesser evil;
our wars were better than their marriages,
ape on she-ape boozing down Saturday night—
home things can't stand up to the strain of the earth.
Now when I wake to their airs of steaks and Ives;
the fade-out classic still lifts my fell of hair—
David once lulled the dark nucleus of Saul—
as you at twelve must, at twenty, fifty, ninety,
young in some summer that has lost my name;
no date I wish you will seem long enough,
if probability is tied to fact—
Only acid seafish think the air is fresh.

3. *End of Camp Alamoosook*

Less than a score, the dregs of the last day,
counselors and campers, man the last arc of island;
the unexpected, the exotic, the early
morning sunlight is more like premature twilight:
last day of the day, foreclosure of the camp.
Glare on the squatting tan, fire of fool's-gold—
like bits of colored glass, it cannot burn.
The Acadians must have gathered in such arcs;
my cousin herded them from Nova Scotia—
no malice, merely working in his line of work,
herding guerrillas in some Morality.
Old Order! The campers harden in their shyness,
their gruff, faint voices hardly say hello,
crying, "Do we love it? *We love it.*"

4. *Familiar Quotations*
(FOR HARRIET)
The poet then, if all else fail, his words from nowhere:
near the ocean, skipping five smooth stones—too happy;
sometimes the little muddler can't stand itself. . . .
Her transistor is singing Anton Webern;
say what it's like? It's hard; if you'll listen to this,
you can listen to anything—it's like red ants,
wild ants, the wild wolf through the woods walking;
the wild spider cry together without tears. . . .
Not this; we want the truth, the very Truth:
he imagined all men were his soul-brother,
boiled the Pharisee in his bloody sweat;
he was all men, he was you, he might have lived;
for love, he threw his lovely youth away—
but you can't love everyone, your heart won't let you.

5. Mink

In the unspoiled age, when they caught a cow-mink,
they made her urinate around the traps,
and every bull-mink hunting along the stream
fell in the trap, and soon the mink were done—
the last we heard of was a freeze in the 50's,
the last bull making tracks in the snow for a last cow.
My friend, once professional, no longer traps:
"We've too many ways to make a living now"—
his a veteran's pension, and two working sons.
He builds houses for bluebirds, martins and swallows.
When a pair mates in one, it's like a catch,
like trapping something—he's sent, it's like a conversion,
China's lost will to excel without improving. . . .
His money goes to *Wildlife;* he killed too much.

6. Cattle

The moon, invisible behind a cloud-ledge,
briefly glitters its bonfire on the harbor. . . .
Machiavelli despised these furiously fought
mounted Tuscan mercenary battles:
lines rushed, and Greek met Greek; one man was killed,
men died of a stroke, but not the strokes of battle.
Our police hit more to terrorize than kill:
a hundred riots, nobody left dead;
clubs break and brains, women are rooked on curbs—
none killed or crippled visibly forever.
Is this tidal wave blown from a bubble of soap?
Why do we always undersell the weak?
Cattle have guts, but after the barn is burned,
they will look at the sunset and tremble.

7. *The Going Generation*

Our going generation; there are days
of pardon . . . perhaps to go on living in
the old United States of William James,
its plaintive, now arthritic, optimism—
hear the swallow's coloratura cheep and cluck,
shrilling underneath its racket, *fuck;*
the feeder dealing out his catfood like cards
to yearling salmon in their stockpond by the falls.
Grace-days . . . It is less than heaven, this dwindling
bulkhead of lawn bristling with binoculars,
overlooking the moon and ocean rising . . .
earth an eyelash on the rim of the lens—drink, drink, see
the rings of Saturn horseshoe round the light-globe. . . .
Some alternatives have no answer; time must answer.

8. *Castine Harbor*

Mostly it's a color; its change and yield
give easily, no stand except the headland:
one substance everywhere divisible;
bosom of freedom, it floats us—less and less
usable now we can fly like the angels.
Yet who would stay alive without the ocean?
Shall we boast marriage is like the ocean:
two parts hydrogen searching for oxygen—
as if the formula existed everywhere
in the numinous Parnassus of chemistry?
The statesman mutters, "The problems of politics
are nothing. . . ." He was thinking of his marriage—
no varnish, changing, the sea is marriage; God is
H_2O Who must forgive us for having lived.

9. *Joy*

On the great day, when the eyelid of life lifts—
why hide it? Joy has had the lion's share;
then, as Ezra Pound said, "Amy Lowell is
no skeleton to hide in your closet." Poor flesh—
the red leaves ember in the blue cool of fall,
the hour, the half hour, before the whiskey hooks,
the humor, the loyalty, the seductive verb,
mouth like a twat, vagina like a jaw,
small-mouth bass shaking the treble hooks. . . .
Descending back into *contemptu mundi,*
I sit, stood-up, in the wrong restaurant,
ringing spare change like sleighbells in my pocket,
fulfilling the prophecy of my first prize,
a field cup won for catching snakes and moths.

10. *Nature*

The circular moon saw-wheels up the oak-grove;
below it, clouds—a permanent of clouds,
many as the waves of the Atlantic, and as shingled.
It makes men nobler to sleep with the sublime,
the Magna Mater had, shivering under oak, moon and cloud.
Such cures the bygone Reichian prophets swore to,
such did as gospel for those virgin times—
two elements were wanting: man and nature.
By sunrise, the show has shifted. Strings of fog,
such as we haven't seen in fifteen months,
catch shyly over lobsterboats and island:
smoke-dust the Chinese draftsman made eternal.
His drawing wears; the hand decayed. A hand does—
we can have faith, at least, the hand decayed.

11. *Growth*
(FOR HARRIET)
"I'm talking the whole idea of life, and boys,
with Mother; and then the heartache, when we're fifty. . . .
You've got to call your next book, *Book of the Century,*
but it will take you a century to write,
then I will have to continue it, when you die."
Latin, Spanish, swimming half a mile,
writing a saga with a hero named Eric,
Latin, Spanish, math and rollerskates;
a love of pretty dresses, but not boys;
composing something with the bells of *Boris:*
"UNTITLED, would have to be the name of it. . . ."
You grow apace, you grow too fast apace,
too fast adult; no, not adult, mature.
On the telephone, they say, "We're tired, aren't you?"

12. *The Graduate*
(FOR ELIZABETH)
"Transylvania's Greek Revival Chapel
is one of the best Greek Revival things in the South;
the College's most distinguished graduate
was a naturalist, he had a French name like Audubon.
My sister, Margaret, a one-bounce basketball
player and all-Southern Center, came home
crying each night because of 'Happy' Chandler,
the coach, and later Governor of Kentucky.
Our great big tall hillbilly idiots keep
Kentucky pre-eminent in basketball.
All that! Still, if you are somewhat ill-born,
you feel your soul is not quite first-class. . . ."
Never such shimmering of intelligence,
though the wind was short, and you stopped smoking.

13. *Outlivers*

"If we could slow the world to what it changed
a hundred years ago, or any hundred,
time-stopping handwork farmwork, handmade wars;
God might give us His right to live forever
despite the eroding miracle of science . . ."
"Is everything that much grander than it is?"
"We think so, but the grandeur dropped us here—
no, it's only people we must miss.
The cave-man, retarded epochs like crab and clam,
wept, as we do, his person dead." We talk
like room-mates bleeding out night to dawn,
each crowds the others to outlive us all—
"But you and Harriet are perhaps like countries
not yet ripe for self-determination."

14. *My Heavenly Shiner*
(FOR ELIZABETH)

The world atop our heads in Maine is north,
zeroes through Newfoundland and Hudson Bay:
entremets chinois et canadiens.
A world like ours will tumble on our heads,
my heavenly Shiner, think of it curving on;
you quiver on my finger like a small
minnow robbed from a small robbed globe,
flittering radiance of my flittering finger.
The fish, the shimmering fish, they go in circles,
not one of them will make it to the Pole—
this isn't the point though, this is not the point;
think of it going on without a life—
in you, God knows, I've had the earthly life—
we were kind of religious, we thought in images.

15. *It Did*

Knowledge, we've had it; our character, the public's—
and yet we will mature, and know we once
did most things better, not just physical
acts, moral: bunking in too high for love,
living twenty-four hours in shirt and drawers,
breathless short hauls, the breathless singles' service;
we could have done much worse. We hope we did
a hundred thousand things much worse! Poor *X*'s,
chance went this way, that way with us here:
gain scored off loss, loss off gain: our tideluck—
it did to live with, but finally all men worsen;
at best, a senile saint, a trap of honey;
at worst, old jaw that bites the hand that fed it,
corruption serenades the wilting tissue.

16. *Seals*

If we must live again, not us; we might
go into seals, we'd handle ourselves better:
able to dawdle, able to torpedo,
all too at home in our double elements,
our third of rocks and ledges. Caught in heaven,
flippering the harbor, blots and patches and oilslick,
so much bluer than water, we think it sky.
Creature could face creator in this suit,
fishers of fish not men. Some other August,
the easy seal might say, "I could not sleep
last night; suddenly I could write my name."
Then all seals preternatural, like us;
take direction, head north—their haven
green ice in a greenland never grass.

(148)

Father and Sons

1. *For Michael Tate: August 1967–July 1968*

Each night, a star, gold-on-black, a muskellunge,
dies in the highest sphere that never dies. . . .
Things no longer possible to our faith
go on routinely usable in nature;
the worst is the child's death. Even his stone,
the very, very old one, one century, two,
his one-year date common in auld lang syne
is no longer for faith's eye-scale. And, Michael Tate,
gagging on your plastic telephone,
while the one night sitter drew water for your bath,
unable to hear your groans. . . . They think: if there'd been
a week or two's illness, we might have been prepared. . . .
Your twin crawls for you, ten-month twin. They are no longer
young enough to understand what happened.

2. *Letter from Allen Tate*

This winter to watch the child of your old age;
and write, "He is my captor. As a young man,
I was too alert to let myself enjoy
my daughter's infancy as I do the little boy's."
Ah that was the mosses ago in your life, mine;
no more eastern flights this season. "As you must guess,
we're too jittery to travel after Michael's death."
You are still magisterial and cocky as when
you gave us young romantics your directive,
"Just shoot when you get the chance, then shoot to kill."
Who else would sire twin sons at sixty-eight?
How sweet your life in retirement! What better than loving
a young wife and boy; without curses writing,
"I shall not live long enough to 'see him through.' "

The End

1. Dies Irae, *A Hope*

"The day this day of wrath will do the world,"
sings Sibyl on snow, sings David *guerrillero,*
"the judge is a hood, canaries sing in torture;
God shoots down everything, even what don't move."
God and our King of greatest majesty,
you who save those you must save free; you, whose
least anger makes our worst a derelict,
have descended from the hills for us,
kept walking to and fro for us on earth;
how often seeking us here you fell dead! . . .
Everything points to non-existence except existence—
on this day, the day God sees the world was good,
this day of the sinful man who must be judged—
good reason to pardon him, good reason to pardon.

2. *On the Border*

"Is Mao's China nearer the Utopia?"
"Only by twelve or fifteen dynasties;
Mao still thinks it dishonorable to carry
firearms except for the birds, war and mobs."
"Are we altogether certain of that much here?
Is even Mao Establishment set to go down fanged,
old king-ape of the ape horde preferring injustice to violence?"
"High culture is lying with an American girl
on the Canadian border, the longest border on earth,
each man there noble as the Queen but not so rich."
"None will abandon his cell to lay a virgin."
"Friends are such a good thing we should cry welcome,
welcome, even if they come from hell . . ."
"There's a strong shadow where there's much light."

For John Berryman

I feel I know what you have worked through, you
know what I have worked through—these are words. . . .
John, we used the language as if we made it.
Luck threw up the coin, and the plot swallowed,
monster yawning for its mess of pottage.
Ah privacy, as if you wished to mount
some rock by a mossy stream, and count the sheep—
fame that renews the soul, but not the heart.
The ebb tide flings up wonders: rivers, beer-cans,
linguini, bloodstreams; how merrily they gallop
to catch the ocean—Hopkins, Herbert, Thoreau,
born to die like the athletes at early forty—
Abraham lived with less expectancy,
heaven his friend, the earth his follower.

Close the Book

The book is finished and the air is lighter,
I can recognize people in the room;
I touch your pictures, find you in the round.
The cat sits pointing the window from the bedspread,
hooked on the nightlife flashing through the curtain;
he is a *dove* and thinks the lights are pigeons—
flames from the open hearth of Thor and Saul,
arms frescoed on the vaults of the creeping cavern,
missiles no dialectician's hand will turn,
fleshspots for the slung chunks of awk and man.
Children have called the anthropoid, father;
he'd stay home Sunday, and they walked on eggs. . . .
The passage from lower to upper middle age
is quicker than the sigh of a match in the water—
we too were students, and betrayed our hand.

Half a Century Gone

(FOR ELIZABETH)

1

We can go on, if free to leave the earth;
our blood, too high, resumes the mortal coil,
hoping past hope to round the earth of Greenbeard,
our springtide's circlet of the fickle laurel,
a funeral wreath from the Despotic Gangster.
I feel the woven cycles of His pain,
reticulations of His spawning cells,
the intimations of my family cancer.
With us, no husband could sit out a marriage.
Those black-bordered letters were like stamps from Turkestan!—
the widows rushed them out, but who received them?
Everyone is dead who signed her name,
almost everyone who cared to answer.
Where are they? They had horses, the gods of the city. . . .

2

Those serfs with the pageboy bob of Shakespeare's kings,
enameled with joy, or speechless with affliction,
are like this summer's landscape chilling under
the first influence of the evening star,
winking from green to black—the body, black
before we even knew that we were dead.
And neither of us the wiser or kinder—torn
darlings, professional sparring partners; and
but for the impossible love, a loyalty
beyond abasement, outside anywhere:
all icy pandemonium. Beatrice
always met us too early or too late,
piercing the firelit hollow of the marriage—
some brightest prong, antennae of the ant. . . .

3

And here on this wavy earth, we, like the others,
too thoughtful clods, may learn from those we walk on:
Star-nosed moles, their catatonic tunnels
and barrows . . . only in touch with what they touch;
blind fur, in mourning, black from shying at limelight,
not as we would, or the lowest serf—
vegetating and protective creatures,
forever falling short of our shortest life.
Through my fieldglasses, I aggrandize
a half-fledged robin with a speckled breast,
big as a pheasant. . . . The invincible
syllogism advances from talon to talon;
no earthly ripple disturbs the ballbearing
utility of the bald and nearest planet. . . .

4

We will remember then our tougher roots:
forerunners hooped to the broiling soil,
until their backs were branded with the coin
of Alexander, small hexagonal sores—
as if they were stretched on burning chicken wire,
skin cooked red and hard as a rusted tin can
by the footlights of the sun—Tillers of the desert!
Think of them, afraid of violence,
afraid of anything, timid as sheep
hidden in some casual, protective crevice,
hollow-eyed, twelve dynasties, to the burning glass,
laid by the sanddrifts of Cleopatra—
what were once identities simplified
to a single, indignant, collusive grin.

(154)

5

On the rainy outlook, the great shade is drawn,
my window, five feet wide, is cracked a foot,
one foot of view blanked out by blind brick.
Domestic gusts of noonday Sunday cooking;
black snow grills on the fire-escape's blacker iron,
Isaiah's living coal. I too, a Sunday prophet,
hear dead sounds ascending, the fertile stench
of horsedroppings from the war-year of our birth.
Fifty-one years, how many millions gone—
this same street, West Sixty-Seven, was here then,
and this same building, the last gasp of true
Nineteenth Century Capitalistic Gothic—
horsedroppings and drippings . . . hear it, hear the clopping
of the hundreds of horses unstopping . . . each hauls a coffin.

Obit

In the end it gets us, though the man know what he'd have:
old cars, old money, old undebased pre-Lyndon
silver, no copper rubbing through . . . old wives;
I could live such a too long time with mine.
In the end, every hypochondriac is his own prophet.
Before the final coming to rest, comes rest
of all transcendence in a mode of being, stopping
all becoming. I'm for and with myself in my otherness,
in the eternal return of earth's fairer children,
the lily, the rose, the sun on dusk and brick,
the loved, the lover, and their fear of life,
their unconquered flux, insensate oneness, their painful "it was . . ."
After loving you so much, can I forget
you for eternity, and have no other choice?

Afterthought

NOTEBOOK 1967–68: as my title intends, the poems in this book are written as one poem, jagged in pattern, but not a conglomeration or sequence of related material. It is not a chronicle or almanac; many events turn up, many others of equal or greater reality do not. This is not my diary, my confession, not a puritan's too literal pornographic honesty, glad to share private embarrassment, and triumph. The time is a summer, an autumn, a winter, a spring, another summer; here the poem ends, except for turned-back bits of fall and winter 1968. I have flashbacks to what I remember, and notes on old history. My plot rolls with the seasons. The separate poems and sections are opportunist and inspired by impulse. Accident threw up subjects, and the plot swallowed them—famished for human chances.

I lean heavily to the rational, but am devoted to surrealism. A surrealist might not say, "The man entered a house," but, "The man entered a police-whistle," or "Seasick with marital happiness, the wife plunges her eyes in her husband swimming like vagueness on the grass." Or make some bent generalization: "Weak wills command the gods." Or more subtly, words that seem right, though loosely in touch with reason: "Saved by my anger from cruelty." Surrealism can degenerate into meaningless clinical hallucinations, or worse into rhetorical machinery, yet it is a natural way to write our fictions.

My opening lines are as hermetic as any in the book. The "fractions" mean that my daughter, born in January, is each July, a precision important to a child, something and a half years old. The "Seaslug etc." are her declining conceptions of God.

I have taken from many books, used the throwaway conversational inspirations of my friends, and much more that I idly spoke to myself. I have no wish to sleuth down my plagiarisms, but want to say that "Hell" is taken from two paragraphs of Glenn Gray's "The Warrior"; ideas and expressions in "Half a Century Gone" come from Simone Weil; ideas and expressions in "Obit" and another poem, from Herbert Marcuse. Two poems steal distortedly from the Urdu poet, Ghalib, literally translated by Aijaz Ahmad. The intelligent and not the stupid quote belongs to R. P. Blackmur in the poem dedicated to him. The borrowings from Plutarch, Sir Thomas More's son-in-law, Emerson, Coleridge, Goethe, Sir Kenneth Clark and Stonewall Jackson are easier to spot.

My meter, fourteen line unrhymed blank verse sections, is fairly strict at first and elsewhere, but often corrupts in single lines to the freedom of prose. Even with this license, I fear I have failed to avoid the themes and gigantism of the sonnet.

A poet can be intelligent and on to what he does; yet he walks, half-balmy, and over-accoutered—caught by his gentle amnesia, his rude ignorance, his too meticulous education. I had good guides when I began. They have gone on with me; by now the echoes are so innumerable that I almost lack the fineness of ear to distinguish them.

In truth I seem to have felt mostly the joys of living; in remembering, in recording, thanks to the gift of the Muse, it is the pain.

ROBERT LOWELL

Winter 1969

Dates

Dates fade faster than we do. Many in the last two years are already gone; in a year or two, most of the rest will slip. I list the few that figure either directly or obliquely in my text:

THE VIETNAM WAR, 1967.

THE ARAB-ISRAELI SIX DAYS' WAR, first week in June 1967.

THE BLACK RIOTS IN NEWARK AND ELSEWHERE, July and August 1967.

CHE GUEVARA's DEATH, October 8, 1967.

THE PENTAGON MARCH, October 21, 1967.

EUGENE MCCARTHY's CAMPAIGN FOR THE DEMOCRATIC NOMINATION, November 1967–August 1968.

ROBERT KENNEDY's CAMPAIGN FOR THE DEMOCRATIC NOMINATION, February 1968–June 1968.

MARTIN LUTHER KING's MURDER, April 4, 1968.

THE COLUMBIA STUDENT DEMONSTRATIONS, April 23 into May 1968.

THE FRENCH STUDENTS' AND WORKERS' UPRISINGS, May 2 into June 1968.

ROBERT KENNEDY's MURDER, June 5, 1968.

THE REPUBLICAN CONVENTION IN MIAMI, August 5–9, 1968.

THE RUSSIAN OCCUPATION OF CZECHOSLOVAKIA, August 21, 1968.

THE DEMONSTRATIONS AND DEMOCRATIC CONVENTION IN CHICAGO, August 25–29, 1968.

THE VIETNAM WAR, 1968.

FSG CLASSICS